Conservative Wit

Edited by

Robert Golla

Best Wishes

Robert Golla

Sale of this book without a front cover may be unauthorized. If this book is coverless, it may have been reported to the publisher as "unsold or destroyed" and neither the author nor the publisher may have received payment for it.

Copyright © 2010 by Robert Golla
All rights reserved

First Edition
April, 2010

ISBN 1451558155

EAN-13 9781451558159

Typeset and printed in the United States of America.

Introduction

In the course of assembling the present collection, I referenced seventy-odd generic quotation collections from the shelves of bookstores and libraries. An iniquity (not unexpected) soon began to emerge.

The *MacMillan Dictionary of Political Quotations* featured no sayings by Russell Kirk, but three by Noam Chomsky. Economist Milton Friedman – who won a Nobel Prize – has five quotes. Economist John Kenneth Galbraith – who didn't – has seventeen. There were three from Elizabeth Dole and four from Phyllis Schlafly, but forty-two from Eleanor Roosevelt. Dwight Eisenhower just beats her with fifty-three entries, though even taken with Ronald Reagan's sixty-two still doesn't topple FDR's colossal 129.

But Perhaps MacMillan was asleep at the wheel...

The Concise Columbia Dictionary of Quotations starts out admirably, with two entries from Jackie Onassis and four from Clare Boothe Luce; one from Jimmy Carter and two from Eisenhower; fifteen from JFK and sixteen from Abraham Lincoln – but fails the acid test with zero from William F. Buckley, Jr. and thirteen from Gore Vidal. Then the numbers unraveled, with two quotes from Thomas Dewey and three from Gloria Steinem; none from President Ford and two from Vice President Mondale; one from Douglas MacArthur and four from Jane Fonda.

In book after book, the tallies mounted, ever-swaying leftward.

Surely I would find parity in the hallowed pages of *Bartlett's Familiar Quotations*, seventeenth edition, wouldn't I?

There were four H.W. Bush quotes to six Bill Clinton quotes; three Eisenhower's and fourteen Truman's; Milton Friedman (three) still can't catch J.K. Galbraith (nine); ten from Nixon and nineteen from JFK; thirty-two from FDR and... freefall – none from Buckley, Gingrich, Kirk, Krauthammer, Limbaugh, Safire, Sowell, or Whittaker Chambers. The grand dames of the movement, Clare Boothe Luce, Phyllis Schlalfy, Peggy Noonan,

Nancy Reagan, Elizabeth Dole, and Ann Coulter were also bypassed without mention to accommodate Hillary Clinton, that eminent orator, who was allotted three entries.

My object with this book was to compile for the first time humor quotations from the giants of the Republican Party and conservatism in general; to anthologize sayings from the men and women who divined and refined a distinctly American movement, dedicated to individualism and freedom, over more than 150 tumultuous years.

With more than one thousand entries ransomed through labor from undeserved isolation in disparate tomes, *Conservative Wit* will provide hours of enlightenment and entertainment, the indulgence of which should be entirely bipartisan; though the reader can proceed with the assurance that the content – is not.

Robert Golla
March 15, 2010

"As Henry VIII said to each of his wives, 'I won't keep you long.'"
Ronald Reagan

"An intellectual is a man who takes more words than necessary to tell more than he knows."
Dwight Eisenhower

"Everyone concedes that fish will not bite in the presence of representatives of the press."
Herbert Hoover

"Tact is the ability to describe others as they see themselves."
Abraham Lincoln

"I am advising the former President, the governor of Florida, and the President of the United States – I guess you could say I rule the world."
Barbara Bush

"The mystery of government is not how Washington works but how to make it stop."
P.J. O'Rourke

"When they call the roll in the Senate, the senators do not know whether to answer 'present' or 'not guilty.'"
Theodore Roosevelt

"The first lesson of economics is scarcity – there is never enough of anything to satisfy all those who want it. The first lesson of politics is to disregard the first lesson of economics."
Thomas Sowell

"Not all spending initiatives were designed to be immortal."
George H.W. Bush

"One way to cut down on the number of favorite sons would be to decree that the one with the fewest votes at the end of the first ballot would be publicly executed."
William F. Buckley, Jr.

"The nice part about being a pessimist is that you are constantly either proven right or pleasantly surprised."
George Will

"Never use a long word when a diminutive one will do."
William Safire

"Except for the occasional heart attack, I never felt better."
Dick Cheney

"If God would have wanted us to live in a permissive society, He would have given us Ten Suggestions and not Ten Commandments."
Zig Ziglar

"Obviously crime pays, or there'd be no crime."
G. Gordon Liddy

"If you don't say anything, you won't be called upon to repeat it."
Calvin Coolidge

"It is easier to love humanity than to love your neighbor."
Eric Hoffer

"I guess I should warn you, if I turn out to be particularly clear, you've probably misunderstood what I've said."
Alan Greenspan

"Monopoly is a terrible thing, till you have it."
Rupert Murdoch

"Michael Dukakis thinks a foreign market is a place to go for French bread."
Rich Bond

"Secretary Powell and I agree on every single issue that has ever been before this administration except for those instances where Colin's still learning."
Donald Rumsfeld

"I spent several years in a North Vietnamese prison camp, in the dark, fed with scraps. Do you think I want to do that all over again as Vice President of the United States?"
John McCain

"The New York Times editorial page is like a Ouija board that has only three answers, no matter what the question. The answers are – higher taxes, more restrictions on political speech, and stricter gun control."
Ann Coulter

"Would you rather go hunting with Dick Cheney or riding in a car over a bridge with Ted Kennedy? At least Cheney takes you to the hospital."
Rush Limbaugh

"In one generation, we have passed from the free distribution of Gideon Bibles to the free distribution of condoms."
Cal Thomas

"You have a heart – you can be a liberal. Now, couple your heart with your brain, and you can be a conservative."
Glenn Beck

"I am not against hasty marriages, where a mutual flame is fanned by an adequate income."
Will Durant

"An economist is someone who sees something happen in practice and wonders if it'd work in theory."
Ronald Reagan

"A good catchword can obscure analysis for fifty years."
Wendell Willkie

"Those who run too fast into the future sometimes trip over the present."
Dwight Eisenhower

"Marriage is neither heaven nor hell; it is simply purgatory."
Abraham Lincoln

"I believe that sex is one of the most beautiful, natural, wholesome things that money can buy."
Tom Clancy

"The people most likely to know the literal definition of irony are the people least likely to appreciate it in its modern form."
Jonah Goldberg

"Portraits act to remedy in the minds of posterity the libels of snap photographs."
Herbert Hoover

"The British capitalize on their accent when they don't want you to know what they're saying. But if you wake them up at 4 A.M., they speak perfect English, the same as we do."
Henry Kissinger

"When you have got an elephant by the hind leg and he is trying to run away, it's best to let him run."
Abraham Lincoln

"Politics and war are remarkably similar situations."
Newt Gingrich

"I don't read the papers. I won't watch TV. I won't do any of that. But I will vote three or four times."
Barbara Bush

"Careers, like rockets, don't always take off on time."
Gary Sinise

"Being bitten in half by a shark is a compromise with being swallowed whole."
P.J. O'Rourke

"When we were at peace, democrats wanted to raise taxes. Now there's a war, so democrats want to raise taxes. When there was a surplus, democrats wanted to raise taxes. Now that there is a mild recession, democrats want to raise taxes."
Ann Coulter

"If Lincoln were alive today, he'd be turning over in his grave."
Gerald Ford

"Princeton sent me a rejection letter so elegantly worded that I still think of myself as an alumnus."
Newt Gingrich

"I haven't had Jimmy Carter's experience. I wouldn't be caught dead with it."
Ronald Reagan

"Who am I to stone the first cast?"
Walter Winchell

"Any change is resisted because bureaucrats have a vested interest in the chaos in which they exist."
Richard Nixon

"The sky is blue, the grass is green. Get off your ass and join the Marines."
John Wayne

"In Arizona we have so little water that the trees chase the dogs."
Barry Goldwater

"The good news is we're ahead in the polls. The bad news is the election isn't tomorrow."
George W. Bush

"I can take care of my enemies all right, but my goddamn friends, they're the ones keeping me walking the floor nights."
Warren Harding

"I am a man of fixed and unbending principles, the first of which is to be flexible at all times."
Everett Dirksen

"The things Congress does best are nothing and overreacting."
Tom Korologos

"I've never belonged to any political party for more than fifteen minutes."
Fiorello La Guardia

"I stopped believing in Santa Claus when I was six. Mother took me to see him in a department store and he asked for my autograph."
Shirley Temple Black

"I was assailed so bitterly that I hardly knew whether I was running for the presidency or the penitentiary."
Ulysses S. Grant

"Extra-marital sex is frowned on, but extra marital sex is applauded."
George Will

"The only way to make a man trustworthy is to trust him."
Henry Stimson

"Unlike presidential administrations, problems rarely have terminal dates."
Dwight Eisenhower

"You know why there's a Second Amendment? In case the government fails to follow the first one."
Rush Limbaugh

"The only trouble was that I just didn't get enough votes."
Herbert Hoover

"I have enough money to last me the rest of my life, unless I buy something."
Jackie Mason

"Take a couple of euphemisms and call me in the morning."
William Safire

"The celebrity is a person who is known for his well-knownness."
Daniel J. Boorstin

"It is often easier to assemble armies than it is to assemble army revenues."
Benjamin Harrison

"Wars are caused by undefended wealth."
Douglas MacArthur

"If this is coffee, please bring me some tea; but if this is tea, please bring me some coffee."
Abraham Lincoln

"No good deed goes unpunished."
Clare Boothe Luce

"Horace, if this theatre burns, it has got to burn around me."
William Howard Taft

"Washington is the one place where you can't take friendship personally."
Tony Snow

"What I wouldn't give to be seventy again!"
Oliver Wendell Holmes, Jr.

"Golf is a game in which you yell 'Fore!', shoot six, and write down five."
Paul Harvey

"Speak softly and carry a big stick."
Theodore Roosevelt

"There is a certain comfort in waking up and finding that Michael Jackson is still the Big Story. At least it tells you that nothing horrible has happened in the world that would force them to move on to real news."
Pat Sajak

"I am a Ford, not a Lincoln."
Gerald Ford

"For liberal Democrats, it is always more blessed to take and then deceive."
Cal Thomas

"The best minds are not in government. If any were, business would steal them away."
Ronald Reagan

"I support the president one hundred percent – when he's right."
Richard Shelby

"Bill Clinton keeps talking about change. But if his economic policies go into effect, change is all you'll have left in your pockets."
George H.W. Bush

"The more we remove penalties for being a bum, the more bumism is going to blossom."
Jesse Helms

"The academic community has in it the biggest concentration of alarmists, cranks, and extremists this side of the giggle house."
William F. Buckley, Jr.

"The longer I am out of office, the more infallible I appear to myself."
Henry Kissinger

"Bad politicians are sent to Washington by good people who don't vote."
William E. Simon

"Balancing the budget is like going to heaven. Everybody wants to do it, but nobody wants to make the trip."
Phil Gramm

"If stocks are optimistic, then so am I."
Lawrence Kudlow

"It's so cold here in Washington, D.C., that politicians have their hands in their own pockets."
Bob Hope

"A neoconservative is a liberal who has been mugged by reality."
Irving Kristol

"If the United States were truly building an empire, for what earthly reason would it choose South Vietnam as the place for which to lay down lives and treasure?"
Mona Charen

"If I am nominated, I will not run. If I am elected, I will not serve. But if you beg me, I just might reconsider."
Alexander Haig

"I am fiercely loyal to those willing to put their money where my mouth is."
Paul Harvey

"It's not a sin to be rich anymore – it's a miracle."
John Connally

"If man asks for many laws it is only because he is sure that his neighbor needs them; privately he is an un-philosophical anarchist, and thinks laws in his own case superfluous."
Will Durant

"I've never been qualified for anything I've done."
Sonny Bono

"Government doesn't solve problems; it subsidizes them."
Ronald Reagan

"Venice would be a fine city, if it were only drained."
Ulysses S. Grant

"I was raised on neglect, anger, and hate. I was raised the old-fashioned way."
Michael Savage

"There is one thing about being President – nobody can tell you when to sit down."
Dwight Eisenhower

"Blessed are the young, for they shall inherit the national debt."
Herbert Hoover

"Gossip is the art of saying nothing in a way that leaves practically nothing unsaid."
Walter Winchell

"If to be head of Hell is as hard as what I have to undergo here, I could find it in my heart to pity Satan."
Abraham Lincoln

"Baseball is a game of race, creed, and color. The race is to first base. The creed is the rules of the game. The color? Well, the home team wears white uniforms, and the visiting team wears gray."
Joe Garagiola

"Money doesn't make you happy. I now have $50 million but I was just as happy when I had $48 million."
Arnold Schwarzenegger

"When you buy peace at any price it is always on the installment plan."
Richard Nixon

"Think twice about criticizing someone's clothes. What they change into could be tighter and shorter than what they took off."
Barbara Bush

"What used to be called shame and humiliation is now called publicity."
P.J. O'Rourke

"You don't need to have a pool at the White House to get in deep water."
Gerald Ford

"Idealism is fine; but as it approaches reality, the cost becomes prohibitive."
William F. Buckley, Jr.

"Dirksen's Three Laws of Politics. 1. Get elected. 2. Get re-elected. 3. Don't get mad, get even."
Everett Dirksen

"Communists never talk about negotiations unless they are losing."
Richard Nixon

"When asked about his own checkered marital past, Mr. Trump said he had never committed 'an infidelity', a statement that sent Ivana Trump and Marla Maples scrambling to find a dictionary."
Bill O'Reilly

"There were so many candidates on the platform that there were not enough promises to go around."
Ronald Reagan

"Happiness is like a cat – if you coax it or call it, it will avoid you; it won't come. But if you pay no attention to it and go about your business, you will find it rubbing against your legs and jumping into your lap."
William Bennett

"I'm trusting in the Lord and a good lawyer."
Oliver North

"If a man went simply by what he saw, he might be tempted to affirm that the essence of democracy is melodrama."
Irving Babbitt

"Finishing second in the Olympics gets you silver. Finishing second in politics gets you oblivion."
Richard Nixon

"There has never been a statue erected to honor a critic."
Zig Ziglar

"Is supply-side economics finished? Only in the sense that Gen. George S. Patton's army was finished in Germany in May, 1945."
Newt Gingrich

"The first step in good reporting is good snooping."
Matt Drudge

"Some newspapers are fit only to line the bottom of bird cages."
Spiro T. Agnew

"Who could not be moved by the sight of that poor, demoralized rabble – outwitted, outflanked, outmaneuvered by the U.S. military? Yet, given time, I think the press will recover."
James Baker

"We now have a President who tries to save money by turning off lights in the White House, even as he heads toward a staggering addition to the national debt. "LBJ" should stand for Light Bulb Johnson."
Barry Goldwater

"The United Nations is just like football – a series of huddles always followed by outbursts of violence."
George Will

"Eighty percent of married men cheat in America. The rest cheat in Europe."
Jackie Mason

"I have noticed that nothing I never said ever did me any harm."
Calvin Coolidge

"I don't want to know what the law is – I want to know who the judge is."
Roy Cohn

"Pray not for lighter burdens, but for stronger backs."
Theodore Roosevelt

"Death has a tendency to encourage a depressing view of war."
Donald Rumsfeld

"Voters do not decide issues, they decide who will decide issues."
George Will

"Equality is a step down for most women."
Phyllis Schlafly

"No plagiarist can excuse the wrong by showing how much of his work he did not pirate."
Learned Hand

"US politicians routinely vie with each other for the Lil' Abner prize for the most humble, most miserable upbringing."
Charles Krauthammer

"The difference between fiction and reality? Fiction has to make sense."
Tom Clancy

"A taxpayer is someone who works for the federal government but doesn't have to take a civil service examination."
Ronald Reagan

"The Left may be sincere, but they're sincerely wrong."
Sean Hannity

"Neither a wise man nor a brave man lies down on the tracks of history to wait for the train of the future to run over him."
Dwight Eisenhower

"There are lots of people who committed crimes during the year who would not have done so if they had been fishing."
Herbert Hoover

"The best thing about the future is that it comes only one day at a time."
Abraham Lincoln

"In case you haven't been following my opponent's get out the vote campaign, ACORN is helping to register groups previously excluded, overlooked, and underserved – second graders, the deceased, Disney characters. In Florida, they even turned up an ACORN registration form that bore the name of one Mickey Mouse. We're checking the paw prints. Although, I might let that one go, I'm pretty sure the big rat's a Republican."
John McCain

"Can you imagine a man who would jump out of two perfectly good airplanes?"
Barbara Bush

"Drugs have taught an entire generation of English kids the metric system."
P.J. O'Rourke

"No, I'm not a good shot, but I shoot often."
Theodore Roosevelt

"The limits of tyrants are prescribed by the endurance of those whom they oppose."
Frederick Douglass

"Savvy observers occasionally note television's resemblance to the weather: Everybody loves to complain about it, but nobody can do anything to fix it."
Michael Medved

"Recession is when a neighbor loses his job, depression is when you lose yours, and recovery is when Jimmy Carter loses his job."
Ronald Reagan

"Anything that calls itself new is doomed to a short life."
Tom Wolfe

"I'm President of the United States, and I'm not going to eat any more broccoli!"
George H.W. Bush

"I should sooner live in a society governed by the first two thousand names in the Boston telephone directory than in a society governed by two thousand faculty members of Harvard University."
William F. Buckley, Jr.

"What the federal government does, basically, is borrow money from people and mail it to people."
George Will

"I was working in my garden one weekend and realized I needed some extra plants. So, dressed in my grubbies and baseball cap, I went to the nursery to find some plants. When I paid for the stuff, the clerk looked at me quizzically and said: 'Did anyone ever tell you that you look just like John Kyl?' I said: 'Yes.' He said: 'I'll bet it makes you mad, don't it?'."
John Kyl

"This is an impressive crowd — the haves and the have-mores. Some people call you the elites; I call you my base."
George W. Bush

"Alexander Hamilton envisioned the judiciary as the 'least dangerous branch' of the federal government. Things have changed."
Laura Ingraham

"I always find that statistics are hard to swallow and impossible to digest. The only one I can ever remember is that if all the people who go to sleep in church were laid end to end they would be a lot more comfortable."
Martha Taft

"Some are born great, some achieve greatness, and some hire public relations officers."
Daniel J. Boorstin

"Going to war without France is like going duck hunting without your accordion."
Donald Rumsfeld

"I am trying to do two things – be a radical and not be a fool – which, if I am to judge by the exhibitions around me, is a matter of no small difficulty."
James Garfield

"The presumption of innocence only means you don't go right to jail."
Ann Coulter

"Government exists to protect us from each other. We can't afford the government it would take to protect us from ourselves."
Ronald Reagan

"Isn't it harder in politics to defeat a fool, say, than an abler man?"
Thomas Dewey

"He who walks in the middle of the road gets hit from both sides."
George Shultz

"If someone throws a chair at you, hell, you pick up a chair and belt him right back."
John Wayne

"There are two things that are important in politics. The first is money, and I can't remember what the second one is."
Mark Hanna

"We're not supposed to have an established religion in America, but we do, and it's called Darwinism."
Ben Stein

"Clinton has repeatedly insisted that his pardon of Marc Rich was the right thing to do; which should probably tip you off to just how wrong it was."
Dennis Miller

"What are the four things wrong with Soviet agriculture? Spring, summer, winter, and fall."
Ronald Reagan

"The buck starts here."
Alan Greenspan

"When I'm getting ready to reason with a man I spend one-third of my time thinking about myself and what I am going to say – and two-thirds thinking about him and what he is going to say."
Abraham Lincoln

"There ought to be a law against asking a golfer what he shoots."
Dwight Eisenhower

"At a Washington party, it is not enough that the guests feel drunk; they must feel drunk and important."
Tom Wolfe

"A presidential campaign is our regular period of large promises to sufferers of all kind."
Herbert Hoover

"Communism is the opiate of the intellectuals."
Clare Boothe Luce

"A man by himself is in bad company."
Eric Hoffer

"The trouble with Hooker is that he's got his headquarters where his hindquarters ought to be."
Abraham Lincoln

"Sure things seldom are."
Malcolm Forbes

"My piecrust is nothing to write home about."
Barbara Bush

"I don't say embrace trouble. That's as bad as treating it like an enemy. But I do say meet it as a friend, for you'll see a lot of it and had better be on speaking terms with it."
Oliver Wendell Holmes, Jr.

"Henry Clay always said he'd rather be right than President. Now President Johnson has proved it really is a choice."
Gerald Ford

"A lot of people quit looking for work as soon as they find a job."
Zig Ziglar

"Status quo is Latin for the mess we're in."
Ronald Reagan

"Television is to news what bumper stickers are to philosophy."
Richard Nixon

"My brother Bob doesn't want to be in government – he promised Dad he'd go straight."
Barry Goldwater

"Ninety percent of the politicians give the other ten percent a bad name."
Henry Kissinger

"Men who never get carried away should be."
Malcolm Forbes

"Once, many, many years ago, I thought I had made a wrong decision. Of course, it turned out that I had been right all along. But I was wrong to have thought I was wrong."
John Foster Dulles

"Inquiry is fatal to certainty."
Will Durant

"If I'm on the course and lightning strikes, I get inside fast. If God wants to play through, let him."
Bob Hope

"Say what you want about the President, but we know his friends have convictions."
Dick Armey

"There are three periods in life – youth, middle age, and 'how well you look'."
Nelson Rockefeller

"You think you are so smart. I'll tell you how smart I am. I went all the way through USL and I have never read a book all the way through."
Paul Hardy

"The First Amendment is about how we govern ourselves – not about how we titillate ourselves sexually."
Robert Bork

"I'm half Greek and half American Indian, so my dermatologist told me I'll never age."
Angie Harmon

"The way the Kennedys are overrunning Washington it's a good thing it was the Mormon Church and not the Catholic Church that practiced polygamy."
George Romney

"To blame the military for war makes about as much sense as suggesting that we get rid of cancer by getting rid of doctors."
Ronald Reagan

"Washington is a resigning town. Nothing else holds the special excitement of a rumored resignation."
George Shultz

"We spent $3 million to study the DNA of bears in Montana. I don't know if that was a paternity issue or a criminal issue."
John McCain

"Born again? No, I'm not. Excuse me for getting it right the first time."
Dennis Miller

"Years may wrinkle the skin, but to give up interest wrinkles the soul."
Douglas MacArthur

"If I announced today I was buying vanilla ice cream for every child in America, David Bonior would jump up and say: 'He wants them all to have heart attacks.'"
Newt Gingrich

"It is unfortunate we can't buy many business executives for what they are worth and sell them for what they think they are worth."
Malcolm Forbes

"McGovern couldn't carry the South if Rhett Butler were his running mate."
Spiro Agnew

"Golf is a game for people who are not active enough for baseball."
William Howard Taft

"The secret of eternal youth is arrested development."
Alice Roosevelt Longworth

"The congressional voting card is the most expensive credit card in the world."
Newt Gingrich

"The melancholy thing in our public life is the insane desire to get higher."
Rutherford B. Hayes

"When buying and selling are controlled by legislators, the first things to be bought and sold are legislators."
P.J. O'Rourke

"Nine-tenths of wisdom consists of being wise in time."
Theodore Roosevelt

"Before I refuse to take your questions, I have an opening statement."
Ronald Reagan

"Writers can't back off from realism, just as an ambitious engineer cannot back off from electricity."
Tom Wolfe

"If Bill Clinton is an 8-handicap, I'm Bobby Jones."
George H.W. Bush

"It must be recalled that under English socialism, all seven of the deadly sins is unemployment."
William F. Buckley, Jr.

"Liberals are stalwart defenders of civil liberties – provided we're only talking about criminals."
Ann Coulter

"Think of how the crime rate would plummet if the illegal was made legal."
Cal Thomas

"There may be more poetry than justice in poetic justice."
George Will

"When a great many people are unable to find work, unemployment results."
Calvin Coolidge

"The Soviets approach arms control much the same way Andy Warhol approached art – anything you can get away with."
Jack Kemp

"When in doubt, fight."
Ulysses S. Grant

"Change is not a destination, just as hope is not a strategy."
Rudy Giuliani

"I admire Ted Kennedy. How many 59-year-olds do you know who still go to Florida for spring break?"
Patrick Buchanan

"I have a reputation for being strait-laced, but actually I come from a very tough state – Utah. Do you think it's easy raising money from people who are all sober?"
Orrin Hatch

"May those who love us, love us. And those who don't love us, may God turn their hearts. And if He doesn't turn their hearts, may He turn their ankles, so we'll know them by their limping."
Ronald Reagan

"Disparagement of television is second only to watching television as an American pastime."
George Will

"Open each session with a prayer and close it with a probe."
Clarence Brown

"A TV host asked my wife: 'Have you ever considered divorce?' She replied: 'Divorce never, murder often.'"
Charlton Heston

"Mass movements can rise and spread without belief in God, but never without belief in a devil."
Eric Hoffer

"The middle of the road is all of the usable surface. The extremes, right and left, are in the gutters."
Dwight Eisenhower

"Only in Washington does a decrease in the proposed increase equal a spending cut."
Larry Elder

"Luck and genius create large fortunes."
Herbert Hoover

"The acceptance speeches of Bill Clinton and Al Gore, orgies of self-revelation, mark the full Oprahfication of American politics."
Charles Krauthammer

"Liberalism, like a backed-up toilet, offends me."
Michael Savage

"I'm not very keen for doves or hawks. I think we need more owls."
George Aiken

"To those critics who are so pessimistic about our economy, I say, don't be economic girlie men!"
Arnold Schwarzenegger

"I'm seventy-four now. My husband's out of office. If I don't like your question, I'm not going to answer it."
Barbara Bush

"While we do wash our dirty linen in public, most others never wash it."
Herbert Hoover

"If you will refrain from telling any lies about the Republican Party, I'll promise not to tell the truth about the Democrats."
Chauncey Depew

"There ought to be a law against any man who doesn't want to marry Myrna Loy."
Jimmy Stewart

"Giving money and power to government is like giving whiskey and car keys to teenage boys."
P.J. O'Rourke

"I know I am getting better at golf because I am hitting fewer spectators."
Gerald Ford

"The West is a place of straightforward people, a place where people understand what the meaning of the word 'is' is."
George W. Bush

"Hubert Humphrey talks so fast that listening to him is like trying to read Playboy magazine with your wife turning over the pages."
Barry Goldwater

"To err is Truman."
Walter Winchell

"A friendship founded on business is better than a business founded on friendship."
John D. Rockefeller

"Sock it to me!"
Richard Nixon

"I'm more of a man than any liberal."
Ann Coulter

"The reason pandas have reduplicating names like Ling-Ling and Hsing-Hsing is that they can't hear well and zoo keepers have to call them twice."
William Safire

"A pound of pluck is worth a ton of luck."
James Garfield

"The most used phrase in my administration if I were to be President would be 'What the hell you mean we're out of missiles?'"
Glenn Beck

"Back in the day, a pair of tight jeans was enough to earn a girl a bad reputation. Now slutty has gone Main Street."
Linda Chavez

"Seven months ago I could give a single command and 541,000 people would immediately obey it. Today I can't get a plumber to come to my house."
Norman Schwarzkopf

"Liberals claim to want to give a hearing to other views, but then are shocked and offended to discover that there are other views."
William F. Buckley, Jr.

"In times like these, it helps to recall that there have always been times like these."
Paul Harvey

"If I had six hours to chop down a tree, I'd spend the first four sharpening the axe."
Abraham Lincoln

"A judge is just a lawyer who somebody's blessed."
William Bennett

"Mr. Ventura is smart enough to avoid commenting on situations like Kosovo, where professional wrestling has never been televised."
Bill O'Reilly

"Contrary to reports that I took the loss badly, I want to say that I went home last night and slept like a baby – every two hours I woke up and cried."
Bob Dole

"If there's one thing we've learned over the years, it's that when you feed the alligator, it comes right back for the next bite."
Wayne LaPierre

"It is a great advantage to a President, and a major source of safety to the country, for him to know that he is not a great man."
Calvin Coolidge

"I would say that if God was good enough for Albert Einstein, he's good enough for Michael Savage."
Michael Savage

"Reading is like the sex act - done privately, and often in bed."
Daniel J. Boorstin

"There might be water on Mars? Call me when you find oil on Mars, okay?"
Dennis Miller

"Government's view of the economy could be summed up in a few short phrases: If it moves, tax it. If it keeps moving, regulate it. And if it stops moving, subsidize it."
Ronald Reagan

"Trying to reach Washington from Duluth is like trying to reach around Rosie O'Donnell at an all-you-can-eat buffet."
Laura Ingraham

"No public man can be just a little crooked."
Herbert Hoover

"Certitude is not the test of certainty."
Oliver Wendell Holmes, Jr.

"Money won't make you happy… but everybody wants to find out for themselves."
Zig Ziglar

"Sweet praise is like perfume. It's fine if you don't swallow it."
Dwight Eisenhower

"Before I got this honorary doctorate, Senator Mitchell called me 'Mr. Gridlock'. But with this degree, I will insist on being called 'Dr. Gridlock.'"
Bob Dole

"'I am bored' generally means 'I am boring.'"
Dennis Prager

"Every calling is great when greatly pursued."
Oliver Wendell Holmes, Jr.

"Now that I'm the mother of a President, I can say almost anything I want and get away with it."
Barbara Bush

"It may be true that you can't fool all the people all the time, but you can fool enough of them to rule a large country."
Will Durant

"The only case where unlimited diversification seems justified is padlock keys."
Herbert Hoover

"A friend is one who has the same enemies you have."
Abraham Lincoln

"Power is the ultimate aphrodisiac."
Henry Kissinger

"Nothing recedes likes success."
Walter Winchell

"Political pornography is not unlike the sexual kind – difficult to define, but you know it when you see it."
Pat Sajak

"To govern is to aggravate."
George Will

"Whenever a Republican leaves one side of the aisle and goes to the other, it raises the intelligence quotient of both parties."
Clare Boothe Luce

"I'm from Hope, Arkansas – you may have heard of it. All I'm asking is: give us one more chance."
Mike Huckabee

"I prefer to call the most obnoxious feminists what they really are – feminazis."
Rush Limbaugh

"If Andy Mellon takes as good care of the government's money as he does of his own, we'll be all right... he ought to be the greatest Secretary of the Treasury since Alexander Hamilton."
Warren Harding

"Nan Collins, my manager, came from Gary, Indiana and suggested I adopt that name... Good thing she didn't come from Poughkeepsie."
Gary Cooper

"What did the President know, and when did Hillary tell him?"
Alfonse D'Amato

"Asking an incumbent member of Congress to vote for term limits is a bit like asking a chicken to vote for Colonel Sanders."
Bob Inglis

"Inflation is the one form of taxation that can be imposed without legislation."
Milton Friedman

"I was guilty of judging capitalism by its works and socialism by its literature."
Sidney Hook

"When I was fourteen, I was the oldest I ever was… I've been getting younger ever since."
Shirley Temple Black

"Do you remember back in the days when you thought that nothing could replace the dollar? Today it practically has!"
Ronald Reagan

"It's like the lazy preacher who used to write long sermons, and the explanation was – he got to writing and was too lazy to stop."
Abraham Lincoln

"Only death is final – and even then I hope for a reprieve."
Phil Gramm

"I think the reason that some twenty-eight, twenty-nine percent are not comfortable voting for a Mormon is they think they're voting for Harry Reid."
Mitt Romney

"When a man weighs 295 pounds, you have to give him some opportunity to make his legs and muscles move, and golf offers that opportunity."
William Howard Taft

"Capitalism works better than it sounds, while socialism sounds better than it works."
Richard Nixon

"We can be absolutely certain only about things we do not understand."
Eric Hoffer

"The Presidency is nothing but a twenty-ring circus – with a whole lot of bad actors."
Herbert Hoover

"McCarthyism is now McCarthywasm."
Dwight Eisenhower

"If there is anything more satisfying than dedicating a new building, it is dedicating eight new buildings."
Nelson Rockefeller

"Colleges are places where pebbles are polished and diamonds are dimmed."
Robert Green Ingersoll

"Every government is a parliament of whores. The trouble is, in a democracy, the whores are us."
P.J. O'Rourke

"I learned a long time ago in politics, never say never."
Gerald Ford

"Marriage is like pantyhose. It all depends on what you put into it."
Phyllis Schlafly

"There was only one thing fair about their policies: They didn't discriminate; they made everyone miserable."
Ronald Reagan

"When Al Gore gives a fireside chat, the fire goes out."
Bob Dole

"Beneath every cynic there lies a romantic, and probably an injured one."
Glenn Beck

"If you are a conservative and leftists have not tried to smear you as a McCarthyite, racist, sexist, or homophobe, it simply means that, in their estimation, you are not very effective."
David Horowitz

"I only know two tunes. One of them is 'Yankee Doodle Dandy'. The other isn't."
Ulysses S. Grant

"I love the smell of juice boxes in the morning."
Robert Duvall

"Every presidential election I've ever been involved with has been characterized as the dirtiest campaign in history."
Roger Ailes

"Avoid popularity if you would have peace."
Abraham Lincoln

"I've never cancelled a subscription to a newspaper because of bad cartoons or editorials. If that were the case, I wouldn't have any newspapers or magazines to read."
Richard Nixon

"It's been hot here. I was sitting here the other night with a lady who fainted. I don't know whether it was the weather or the conversation."
Calvin Coolidge

"What do I know about sex? I'm a married man."
Tom Clancy

"You have no idea how depressing and fatiguing it is to live in the same house where you work."
Chester Arthur

"People who enjoy meetings should not be in charge of anything."
Thomas Sowell

"You can't talk of the dangers of snake poisoning and not mention snakes."
C. Everett Koop

"In 1957, I spoke for twenty-four hours and eighteen minutes. I could have spoken another twelve hours but I thought twenty-four hours had dramatized the situation sufficiently."
Strom Thurmond

"Censorship, like charity, should begin at home; but unlike charity, it should end there."
Clare Boothe Luce

"Appeasement does not always lead to war; sometimes it leads to surrender."
William Safire

"The nearest thing to eternal life we will ever see on this earth is a government program."
Ronald Reagan

"Practice whatever the big truth is so that you can say it in forty seconds on camera."
Newt Gingrich

"Photographs of me on horseback, yes; tennis, no. And golf is fatal."
Theodore Roosevelt

"The first step of an American entering upon a literary career was to pretend to be an Englishman."
Henry Cabot Lodge

"It is not given even to the Presidents to see the future."
Herbert Hoover

"If you've got them by the balls, their hearts and minds will follow."
John Wayne

"Liberals have invented whole college majors – psychology, sociology, women's studies – to prove that nothing is anybody's fault."
P.J. O'Rourke

"It is best not to swap horses while crossing the river."
Abraham Lincoln

"A law can be both economic folly and constitutional."
Antonin Scalia

"I don't care if he's got two horns and a tail. As long as he's anti-Communist, we can use him."
Douglas MacArthur

"I sometimes find retirement so exhausting that I think I'll get a job."
Barbara Bush

"The President's status varies directly with the Dow Jones Average."
George Will

"Much of man's thinking is propaganda of his appetites."
Eric Hoffer

"One way to make sure crime doesn't pay would be to let the government run it."
Ronald Reagan

"I know a baseball star who wouldn't report the theft of his wife's credit cards because the thief spends less than she does."
Joe Garagiola

"Many teachers now consider the traditional idea of teaching to be intellectually suspect and morally offensive because it is tainted by the authoritarian idea that there are defensible standards and by the in-egalitarian idea that some people do things better than others."
George Will

"This is probably Lyndon Johnson's year, and the Archangel Gabriel running on the Republican ticket probably could not win."
William F. Buckley, Jr.

"Steroids, they're not just for breakfast anymore."
Anita Bryant

"Putting and fishing are two of the things I hate the most."
George H.W. Bush

"I'm not the inventor of negative campaigning, but I'm an ardent practitioner."
Lee Atwater

"There is never enough time, unless you're serving it."
Malcolm Forbes

"If it were not for the reporters, I would tell you the truth."
Chester Arthur

"Moral codes adjust themselves to environmental conditions."
Will Durant

"In the final choice a soldier's pack is not so heavy a burden as a prisoner's chains."
Dwight Eisenhower

"Not all restaurants are equal. There is a parallel to the subject of immigration."
Michael Savage

"I don't know what people have against Jimmy Carter. He's done nothing."
Bob Hope

"I read *The New York Times* and my Bible every day so that I know what each side is doing."
Cal Thomas

"I don't know much about Americanism, but it's a damn good word with which to carry an election."
Warren Harding

"Look, I don't even agree with myself at times."
Jeane Kirkpatrick

"Character is what you are in the dark."
Dwight Moody

"It is said that modern societies alternate between exhilaration about the achieving of progress and disappointment about the fruits of it."
George Will

"A man walked up to me on a Memphis street, slapped me on the back, pumped my hand vigorously and said: 'If I'd know'd you was going to win, I'd of voted for you.'"
Dan Kuykendall

"There is only one quality worse than hardness of heart and that is softness of head."
Theodore Roosevelt

"The difference between the men and the boys is the price of their toys."
Malcolm Forbes

"If enough people openly engage in conduct once considered reprehensible, we rewrite the rule book and assume that God, as a good democrat, will go along."
James L. Buckley

"I've never been able to understand why a Republican contributor is a 'fat cat' and a Democratic contributor of the same amount of money is a 'public-spirited philanthropist.'"
Ronald Reagan

"One time we thought we'd outsmart the crowd. We sent a decoy limousine off in one direction while I snuck out the back entrance. As we rounded the corner, I'll never forget it. I saw one of the ugliest and angriest women I've ever seen in my entire life. Boy she was really bad. And she charged up to my car with a sign. I don't see why the secret service let her up that close. 'Stay out of my womb!' No problem, lady."
George H.W. Bush

"It was once an American tradition to pay off the mortgage and leave the children the farm. Now we seem to be selling the farm and leaving our children the mortgage."
Newt Gingrich

"Wars produce many stories of fiction, some of which are told until they are believed to be true."
Ulysses S. Grant

"I don't think it's particularly smart to spend your time responding to the other candidate."
James Baker

"Heroes may not be braver than anyone else. They're just braver five minutes longer."
Ronald Reagan

"An honest politician is one who, when he is bought, will stay bought."
Simon Cameron

"The great act of faith is when a man decides he is not God."
Oliver Wendell Holmes, Jr.

"I shall always consider it the highest tribute to my administration that the opposition have based so little of their criticism on what I have really said and done."
Calvin Coolidge

"Whenever whom is required, recast the sentence. This keeps a huge section of the hard disk of your mind available for baseball averages."
William Safire

"I don't date rock 'n' rollers. I just marry them."
Heather Locklear

"You cannot defrost a refrigerator with an ax."
Dwight Eisenhower

"A fact without a theory is like a ship without a sail, a boat without a rudder, a kite without a tail."
George Shultz

"If 'pro' is the opposite of 'con' what is the opposite of 'progress?'"
Paul Harvey

"He may not be able to keep a job, but he's certainly never boring."
Barbara Bush

"Make sure that you tell the parliamentarian that I want to keep this an absolute secret. That will get the word around the Hill faster than Western Union."
Gerald Ford

"Here in Hollywood you can actually get a marriage license printed on an Etch-A-Sketch."
Dennis Miller

"Senator Obama is ready for any contingency – even the possibility of a sudden and dramatic market rebound. I'm told that at the first sign of recovery, he will suspend his campaign and fly immediately to Washington to address this crisis."
John McCain

"A good fisherman possesses much faith and hope or he would not fish. He gains even in charity when he listens to other fisherman."
Herbert Hoover

"Few things are as stimulating as other people's calamities observed from a safe distance."
George Will

"It is a little amusing to see the stickers that have been worn by so many of my colleagues that say: "Term Limits, Yes." It doesn't say: "Term Limits, Now." It says: "Term Limits, Yes." I'm reminded of the great and famous prayer of St. Augustine, who said: "Dear God, make me pure. But not now.""
Henry Hyde

"President Dewey warned me not to get overconfident."
Ronald Reagan

"Do I have a great vision to make Louisiana the best state on the country? I don't know."
Jay Blossman

"Good morning, David. Did you do any fornicating this weekend?"
Richard Nixon

"Even in a world where the lion and the lamb are about to lie down together, it is very important that the United States of America be the lion."
Phil Gramm

"It's a great country, where anybody can grow up to be President… except me."
Barry Goldwater

"I've been to war. I've raised twins. If I had a choice, I'd rather go to war."
George W. Bush

"If you treat your wife like a thoroughbred, you'll never end up with a nag."
Zig Ziglar

"I would honor the man who would give to his country a good newspaper."
Rutherford B. Hayes

"I've noticed that everyone that is for abortion has already been born."
Ronald Reagan

"Show me a man who claims he is objective and I'll show you a man with illusions."
Henry Luce

"The surest test of discipline is its absence."
Clara Barton

"Three things have been difficult to tame – the oceans, fools, and women. We may soon be able to tame the oceans; fools and women will take a little longer."
Spiro T. Agnew

"The first time I campaigned, I probably lost George hundreds of votes. I'm not only outspoken, I'm honest."
Barbara Bush

"There is one rule of action more important than all others. It consists in never doing anything that someone else can do for you."
Calvin Coolidge

"I just loaned Bolivia $2 million, but I play $1 Nassaus."
Dwight Eisenhower

"Power means not needing to raise your voice."
George Will

"No man has a good enough memory to make a successful liar."
Abraham Lincoln

"My hobby is work."
Herbert Hoover

"The only really firm rule of taste about cross dressing is that neither sex should ever wear anything they haven't yet figured out how to go to the bathroom in."
P.J. O'Rourke

"I guess a small-town mayor is sort of like a community organizer, except that you have actual responsibilities."
Sarah Palin

"The most successful politician is he who says what everybody is thinking most often and in the loudest voice."
Theodore Roosevelt

"I've learned to mumble with great incoherence."
Alan Greenspan

"I was alarmed at my doctor's report. He said I was sound as a dollar."
Ronald Reagan

"There's nothing like a good dose of another woman to make a man appreciate his wife."
Clare Boothe Luce

"Nothing is easier than spending the public money. It does not appear to belong to anybody."
Calvin Coolidge

"Tonight I'll try to hold my charisma in check."
George H.W. Bush

"Every morning I pray to God to give me the wisdom to do the right thing during the day. Then I ask God: 'Is there anything I can do for you?'"
Henry Kissinger

"A billion here, a billion there, and pretty soon you're talking about real money."
Everett Dirksen

"Every President needs an SOB – and I'm Nixon's."
H.R. Haldeman

"I'm sitting on the fence with both ears firmly planted on the ground."
Dan Marriott

"There is no lie too improbable, no distortion too great, no smear campaign too dirty for the State Department and the media to embrace."
Jesse Helms

"When I was in fifth grade, I'm not sure that I knew what a national debt was. Of course, when I was in the fifth grade, we didn't have one."
Ronald Reagan

"Don't spend time beating on a wall, hoping to transform it into a door."
Laura Schlessinger

"Sometimes in politics one must deal with skunks, but no one should be fool enough to allow the skunks to choose the weapons."
Joseph Cannon

"One man cannot hold another man down in the ditch without remaining down in the ditch with him."
Booker T. Washington

"Most of us spend too much time on the last twenty-four hours and too little on the last six thousand years."
Will Durant

"Americans will respect your beliefs if you just keep them private."
Bill O'Reilly

"When I came to town and saw the price of diesel went above regular gas, that burnt me up."
Ron Ziegler

"If everybody in this town connected with politics had to leave town because of chasing women and drinking, you would have no government."
Barry Goldwater

"I don't initiate violence – I retaliate!"
Chuck Norris

"I'll be glad to reply to or dodge your questions, depending on what I think will help our election most."
George H. W. Bush

"The swing voters – I like to refer to them as the idiot voters because they don't have set philosophical principles. You're either a liberal or you're a conservative if you have an IQ above a toaster."
Ann Coulter

"I hate these white-tie getups. There's just no room for my shoulder holster."
Dick Cheney

"Education is a progressive discovery of our own ignorance."
Will Durant

"I would not say that the future is necessarily less predictable than the past. I think the past was not predictable when it started."
Donald Rumsfeld

"If you could kick the person in the pants responsible for most of your trouble, you wouldn't sit for a month."
Theodore Roosevelt

"I have seen it happen more often than not that when one asks for choices one is always given three: two absurd ones and the preferred one. And the experienced bureaucrat, which I am slowly becoming, can usually tell the preferred one because it is almost always the one that is typed in the middle."
Henry Kissinger

"Today's radical-liberal posturing in the Senate is about as closely related to a Harry Truman as is a Chihuahua to a timber wolf."
Spiro Agnew

"My social security number is 8."
John McCain

"Before I begin, could I ask a favor? Would somebody please keep an eye on my seat?"
Gerald Ford

"In every election in American history both parties have their clichés. The party that has the clichés that ring true wins."
Newt Gingrich

"The other day I gave up my seat in the streetcar, and three ladies sat down."
William Howard Taft

"The expansion of federal activity is a form of eating for politicians."
William F. Buckley, Jr.

"There is only one basic human right, the right to do what you damn well please."
P.J. O'Rourke

"The current tax code is a daily mugging."
Ronald Reagan

"Getting the support of Syria is the moral equivalent of winning the Klan's endorsement – it might be useful but it doesn't necessarily speak well of you."
Jonah Goldberg

"I am amazed that CNN can't get its act together."
Rupert Murdoch

"Labor disgraces no man; unfortunately, you occasionally find men who disgrace labor."
Ulysses S. Grant

"Oh, if I could only be President and Congress, too, for just ten minutes."
Theodore Roosevelt

"President Clinton had a bill, e-i-e-i-o. And in that bill was lots of pork, e-i-e-i-o."
Alfonse D'Amato

"Bean-counting government bureaucrats are free to take race, ethnicity and gender into account when doling out public funds to non-white-male contractors. But God help law enforcement officers, air marshals and border agents who try to use those same factors to combat terrorism and protect American lives."
Michelle Malkin

"Everything Reagan does, Gorbachev does one better. Reagan wears the flag of his country on his lapel, Gorby wears the map of his country on his forehead."
Bob Hope

"Self-appreciation is a cardinal necessity for successful politics."
William F. Buckley, Jr.

"We may divide the struggles of the human race into two chapters – first, the fight to get leisure; and second, what to do with our leisure when we have won it. Like all blessings, leisure is a bad thing unless it is well used."
James Garfield

"Having lost a close one eight years ago, and having won a close one this year, I know winning is a lot more fun."
Richard Nixon

"One and God make a majority."
Frederick Douglass

"Christmas Eve. By this time tomorrow, millions of Americans, knee-deep in tinsel and wrapping paper, will utter those heartfelt words: 'Is this all I got?'"
Kelsey Grammer

"If Al Gore invented the internet, I invented spell check."
Dan Quayle

"If my ancestors had known that Ellis Island was in New Jersey, they might have stayed in Italy."
Rudy Giuliani

"I think it speaks volumes about how little we value basic education in America that only one of the Three R's actually begins with the letter 'R.'"
Dennis Miller

A friend of mine was asked to a costume ball a short time ago. He slapped some egg on his face and went as a liberal economist."
Ronald Reagan

"Good money never made times hard."
William McKinley

"Stupidity often saves a man from going mad."
Oliver Wendell Holmes, Jr.

"Live rich, die poor. Never make the mistake of doing it the other way round."
Walter Annenberg

"Many years ago I concluded that a few hair shirts were part of the mental wardrobe of every man. The President differs only from other men in that he has a more extensive wardrobe."
Herbert Hoover

"Women's Rights: Supporting the right to destroy a fetus for any reason, including personal convenience. Animal Rights: Opposing the right to destroy a rabbit for cancer research."
Dennis Prager

"Palin didn't need Greek columns. People react to her because they believe she represents what the Greeks established."
Kathryn Jean-Lopez

"A muttonhead, after an education at West Point – or Harvard – is a muttonhead still."
Theodore Roosevelt

"I once called Carter a 'chicken-fried McGovern', and I take that back because I've come to respect McGovern."
Bob Dole

"Fame usually comes to those who are thinking about something else."
Oliver Wendell Holmes, Jr.

"Don't ever become a general. If you become a general you just plain have too much to worry about."
Dwight Eisenhower

"Ben Franklin may have discovered electricity – but it is the man who invented the meter who made the money."
Earl Warren

"The individual who has to justify his existence by his own efforts is in eternal bondage to himself."
Eric Hoffer

"People might not get all they work for in this world, but they must certainly work for all they get."
Frederick Douglass

"All I ever did was marry and birth well."
Barbara Bush

"For those who like that sort of thing, I should think that it's just about the sort of thing they would like."
Abraham Lincoln

"You know you're getting old when the candles cost more than the cake."
Bob Hope

"Politics is supposed to be the second-oldest profession. I have come to realize that it bears a very close resemblance to the first."
Ronald Reagan

"Liberals love America like O.J. loved Nicole."
Ann Coulter

"The smart ones ask when they don't know. And, sometimes when they do."
Malcolm Forbes

"It appears we are defeated by the combined power of rebellion, Catholicism, and whiskey – a trinity very hard to conquer."
James Garfield

"Clinton was out, Bush was in. Oral sex was out, oral prayer was in."
Michael Savage

"I would not be truthful if I said I was fully qualified for the office. I do not play the piano, I seldom play golf, and I never play touch football."
Barry Goldwater

"I don't dare ask how many George Bush cards you have to trade to get one Michael Jordan."
George H.W. Bush

"An adage is an old saying. Any 'old adage' is redundant and subject to execution before the squad squad."
William Safire

"Some pols' faces have been pulled so tight it's a wonder they can close their eyes at night."
Laura Ingraham

"My success so far has only been won by absolute indifference to my future career."
Theodore Roosevelt

"Football brings out the sociologist that lurks in some otherwise respectable citizens."
George Will

"Did you mail that cheque to the judge?"
Roy Cohn

"Foreign aid is like opium. There are withdrawal pains if you remove it."
John Foster Dulles

"An expert is somebody who is more than fifty miles away from home, has no responsibility for implementing the advice he gives, and shows slides."
Edwin Meese III

"If an Englishman gets run down by a truck, he apologizes to the truck."
Jackie Mason

"President Carter has been debating candidate Carter for the past three and a half years – and losing."
Ronald Reagan

"A person is always startled when he hears himself seriously called an old man for the first time."
Oliver Wendell Holmes, Jr.

"They say marriages are made in Heaven, but so are thunder and lightning."
Clint Eastwood

"Tonight I am a private citizen. Tomorrow, I shall be called to assume new responsibilities and, on the day after, the broadside of the world's wrath will strike."
James Garfield

"If you can't say anything good about someone, sit right here by me."
Alice Roosevelt Longworth

"Hell hath no fury like the bureaucrat scorned."
Milton Friedman

"It's a great pleasure to be at the Yale Law School Sesquicentennial Convocation… and I defy anyone to say that and chew gum at the same time."
Gerald Ford

"Once upon a time my political opponents honored me as possessing the fabulous intellectual and economic power by which I could create a worldwide Depression all by myself."
Herbert Hoover

"Gossip is what you say about the objects of flattery when they aren't present."
P.J. O'Rourke

"The older you get, the farther from the camera you need to be."
Heather Locklear

"When one gets in bed with government, one must expect the diseases it spreads."
Ron Paul

"Diamonds are nothing more than chunks of coal that stuck to their jobs."
Malcolm Forbes

"An atheist is a guy who watches a Notre Dame – SMU football game and doesn't care who wins."
Dwight Eisenhower

"God must love the common man, he made so many of them."
Abraham Lincoln

"Osama Bin Laden is either alive and well, or alive and not too well, or not alive."
Donald Rumsfeld

"There is a myth around I don't dress well. I dress very well – I just don't look so good."
Barbara Bush

"It does not affect your daily life very much if your neighbor marries a box turtle. But that does not mean it is right."
John Cornyn

"History is no easy subject. Even in my day it wasn't, and we had so much less to learn then."
Ronald Reagan

"Arnold Schwarzenegger's gubernatorial campaign raises a series of fascinating questions, the most perplexing of all being why an international star of his stature would ever want to run in the first place."
Michael Medved

"The chief idea of the American people is idealism."
Calvin Coolidge

"One reason that even many heroes of the past no longer seem quite so heroic is that the art of biography has changed for the better."
George Will

"If power made one evil, then God would be the Devil."
Jonah Goldberg

"A recent police study found that you're much more likely to get shot by a fat cop if you run."
Dennis Miller

"In the history of the nation, there has never been a political party so ridiculous as today's democrats. It's as if all the brain-damaged people in America got together and formed a voting bloc."
Ann Coulter

"A spirit of national masochism prevails, encouraged by an effete corps of impudent snobs who characterize themselves as intellectuals."
Spiro Agnew

"For years politicians have promised the moon – I'm the first one to be able to deliver it."
Richard Nixon

"I've still got a lot to learn about Washington. Why, yesterday I accidentally spent some of my own money."
Fred Thompson

"Nature has never read the Declaration of Independence. It continues to make us unequal."
Will Durant

"I get satisfaction of three kinds. One is creating something, one is being paid for it, and one is the feeling that I haven't just been sitting on my ass all afternoon."
William F. Buckley, Jr.

"I thought the Secret Service would protect me from the press, but they were at my house to protect me from assassins with guns, not from assassins with pencils."
Michael Reagan

"Sooner or later all politicians die of swallowing their own lies."
Clare Boothe Luce

"I think we all agree, the past is over."
George W. Bush

"When I feel like exercising, I just lie down until the feeling goes away."
Robert M. Hutchins

"In a battle between corporate profits and the environment, the environment has about as much a chance of coming out on top as Pat Buchanan does of winning a Soul Train lifetime achievement award."
Dennis Miller

"The first ladyship is the only federal office in which the holder can neither be fired nor impeached."
William Safire

"On the theory of the tobacco precedent, car manufacturers should be liable for deaths caused by speed."
Robert Bork

"Many marriages would be better if the husband and the wife clearly understood that they are on the same side."
Zig Ziglar

"The nine most terrifying words in the English language are: 'I'm from the government and I'm here to help you.'"
Ronald Reagan

"It was said of Ronald Reagan that he had so much respect for the presidency he never removed his suit coat while in the Oval Office. Clinton respects it so little he has trouble keeping his pants on there."
Cal Thomas

"Let them march all they want, as long as they continue to pay their taxes."
Alexander Haig

"Politicians employ speechwriters as ventriloquists."
George Will

"Very few of the early Italian humanists were really humane."
Irving Babbitt

"Senator Kerry says he sees two Americas. And that makes the whole thing mutual – America sees two John Kerrys."
Dick Cheney

"You can criticize me, but don't criticize my children and don't criticize my daughters-in-law and don't' criticize my husband, or you're dead."
Barbara Bush

"When individuals enter upon a foolish project they pay for it, but if the government does the same thing, both the foolish and the wise must pay for it."
Herbert Hoover

"There are only two ways of telling the complete truth – anonymously and posthumously."
Thomas Sowell

"We have the same percentage of lightweights in Congress as you have in your hometown. After all, it's representative government."
Alan Simpson

"No matter how much cats fight, there always seem to be plenty of kittens."
Abraham Lincoln

"People are not complete fools (though you might not always be able to recognize this from the editorials of *The New York Times*)."
Mona Charen

"The line between idiosyncrasy and idiocy is money."
Malcolm Forbes

"An intellectual is a man who doesn't know how to park a bike."
Spiro Agnew

"Nobody believes the official spokesman, but everybody trusts an unidentified source."
Ron Nessen

"The Democratic Party is not one, but two political parties with the same name. They unite only once every two years – to wage political campaigns."
Dwight Eisenhower

"An optimist is someone who goes after Moby Dick in a rowboat and takes the tartar sauce with him."
Zig Ziglar

"My cholesterol's lower than Clinton's, my blood pressure's lower than Clinton's, my weight is less than Clinton's. I am not going to make health an issue."
Bob Dole

"The business of America is business."
Calvin Coolidge

"I've laid down the law to everyone from now on about anything that happens that no matter what time it is I'm to be awakened, even if it's in the middle of a cabinet meeting."
Ronald Reagan

"I was an oilman who never made a million, a lawyer who never had a case, and a politician who carried only Maine and Vermont."
Alf Landon

"Liberalism is a mental disorder."
Michael Savage

"Honesty is the best policy, even when running for Congress."
James Garfield

"Bryan is a personally honest and rather attractive man, a real orator and a born demagogue, who has every crank, fool, and putative criminal in the country behind him, and a large proportion of the ignorant honest class."
Theodore Roosevelt

"People who bite the hand that feeds them usually lick the boot that kicks them."
Eric Hoffer

"No nation or individual has been able to squander itself into prosperity."
Herbert Hoover

"I write to discover what I think. After all, the bars aren't open that early."
Daniel J. Boorstin

"If I owe Smith ten dollars and God forgives me, that doesn't pay Smith."
Robert Green Ingersoll

"Our government is the most successful contrivance the world has ever known for preventing things from being done."
Charles Evans Hughes

"In the Middle Ages it was the fashion to wear hair shirts to remind one's self of trouble and sin. Many years ago I concluded that a few hair shirts were part of the mental wardrobe of every man. The President differs only from other men in that he has a more extensive wardrobe."
Herbert Hoover

"Entitlement spending – the politics of greed wrapped in the language of love."
Dick Armey

"I have come up with a new national symbol for the United States. I think we need to junk the eagle and come up with a symbol that is more appropriate for the kind of government we have today. We need to replace the eagle with a huge sow that has a lot of nipples and a bunch of fat little piglets hanging on them, all trying to suckle as much nourishment from them as possible."
Rush Limbaugh

"Because of their size, parents may be difficult to discipline properly."
P.J. O'Rourke

"I was America's first instant Vice President – and now, America's first instant President. The Marine Corps Band is so confused, they don't know whether to play 'Hail to the Chief' or 'You've Come a Long Way, Baby.'"
Gerald Ford

"Labels are for cans."
George H.W. Bush

"I rise only to say that I do not intend to say anything."
Ulysses S. Grant

"A man's home may seem to be his castle on the outside; inside it is more often his nursery."
Clare Boothe Luce

"A conservative is a man who will not change things until he studies things. The radical wants to change regardless."
Robert Taft

"It's so much easier to suggest solutions when you don't know too much about the problem."
Malcolm Forbes

"My idea of fast food is a mallard."
Ted Nugent

"Heaven help us if government ever gets into the business of protecting us from ourselves."
Ronald Reagan

"Washington is… a city of cocker spaniels. It's a city of people who are more interested in being petted and admired, loved, than rendering the exercise of power."
Elliot Richardson

"Nobody will ever win the battle of the sexes. There's too much fraternizing with the enemy."
Henry Kissinger

"You can't inflate your way to economic growth."
Jack Kemp

"The best executive is the one who has sense enough to pick good men to do what he wants done, and self-restraint enough to keep from meddling with them while they do it."
Theodore Roosevelt

"Reduce the number of lawyers. They are like beavers – they get in the middle of the stream and dam it up."
Donald Rumsfeld

"The War Department moves in mysterious ways."
Dwight Eisenhower

"Pro football gave me a great sense of perspective to enter politics. I'd already been booed, cheered, cut, sold, traded, and hung in effigy."
Jack Kemp

"I have rather a yen for fishing because the ripple of a brook and the slap of a wave against the side of a boat will brainwash most anybody into a much clearer position."
Herbert Hoover

"Cutting the heart out of our defenses for the next several years is roughly like canceling all your fire insurance because you did not have a fire last year."
Caspar Weinberger

"That some should be rich shows that others may become rich."
Abraham Lincoln

"You could say I grew up in a *Lord of the Flies* neighborhood."
Michael Savage

"I never did care much for the upholstery of office."
James Garfield

"One office employee said to another, watching a filled dumpster going by in a hallway: 'I love the smell of shredded documents in the morning.'"
Lynne Cheney

"Honey, I forgot to duck!"
Ronald Reagan

"It's a good rule never to send a mouse to catch a skunk or a polliwog to tackle a whale."
Abraham Lincoln

"What a blessed thing it is that Nature, when she invented, manufactured, and patented her authors, contrived to make critics out of the chips that were left!"
Oliver Wendell Holmes, Jr.

"When it comes to betting on yourself... you're a chicken-livered coward if you hesitate."
B.C. Forbes

"If hypocrisy were gold, the Capital would be Fort Knox."
John McCain

"George Bush sleeps with two girls. Millie and me."
Barbara Bush

"Nine-tenths of wisdom consists in being wise in time."
Theodore Roosevelt

"People say I'm arrogant, but I know better."
John Sununu

"A bronco is something that kicks and bucks, twists and turns, and very seldom goes in one direction. We have one of those things here in Washington – it's called the Congress."
Gerald Ford

"The press is like the peculiar uncle you keep in the attic – just one of those unfortunate things."
G. Gordon Liddy

"Carter said he'd do something about unemployment. He did. In April, 825,000 Americans lost their jobs."
Ronald Reagan

"On 106 occasions, bribes were offered or discussed. On 105 of those occasions, the public official involved accepted the bribe. And on the other occasion he turned it down because he didn't think the amount was enough."
Rudy Giuliani

"Forget that I am President of the United States. I am Warren Harding, playing with some friends, and I'm going to beat the hell out of them."
Warren Harding

"I have great expectations for the future, because the past was highly overrated."
Sylvester Stallone

"The democrats would much rather project pictures of starving children than keep children from starving, provided they can blame the republicans."
William F. Buckley, Jr.

"Pessimism is as American as apple pie – frozen apple pie with a slice of processed cheese."
George Will

"I'm not particularly sensitive. I've been called almost everything. But please don't call me Hubert."
Richard Nixon

"I not only have no skeletons – I have no closet."
Oliver North

"Anyone who has seen me spin that heavy, giant wheel on television knows that I'm not a steroid user."
Pat Sajak

"I'm carrying so much pork, I'm beginning to get trichinosis."
Phil Gramm

"We are told God is dead. Well, he isn't. We just can't talk to Him in the classroom anymore."
Ronald Reagan

"The House maintains a barbershop, where congressmen pay fifty cents for a haircut, but custom dictates that they tip an additional fifty cents, so it costs them a dollar. The Senate is different. You get the haircut free, but the traditional tip is a dollar. So, you see, the haircut is as free as most things furnished by the government."
Norris Cotton

"Don't hit a man if you can possibly avoid it; but if you do hit him, put him to sleep."
Theodore Roosevelt

"I thought Deep Throat was a movie about a giraffe."
Bob Hope

"Four-fifths of all our troubles would disappear, if we would only sit down and keep still."
Calvin Coolidge

"I can't wish my opponent luck, but I do wish him well."
John McCain

"The next time some academics tell you how important diversity is, ask how many republicans there are in their sociology department."
Thomas Sowell

"I always feel a genuine bond whenever I see Senator Clinton. She's the only person who's at the center of more conspiracy theories than I am."
Dick Cheney

"When I hear a man preach, I like to see him act as if he were fighting bees."
Abraham Lincoln

"It's going to be a bummer if Mars turns out to be like us."
Newt Gingrich

"If you say a modern celebrity is an adulterer, a pervert, and a drug addict, all it means is that you've read his autobiography."
P.J. O'Rourke

"My grandfather always said: 'Don't watch your money; watch your health.' So one day while I was watching my health, someone stole my money. It was my grandfather."
Jackie Mason

"My dear Kathleen, you were saved a lot of trouble by not being born earlier. I'm glad you want to be a doctor and not President. We do not have enough doctors, and there seems to be a sufficient number of candidates for President."
Herbert Hoover

"Social position is now more a matter of press than prestige."
Walter Winchell

"Somewhere out in this audience may even be someone who will one day follow in my footsteps and preside over the White House as the President's spouse. I wish him well."
Barbara Bush

"It is the hallmark of the expert professional that he doesn't care where he is going as long as he proceeds competently."
Herman Kahn

"Plutography: Depicting the acts of the rich."
Tom Wolfe

"It's really difficult to go out on a date with the secret service."
Julie Nixon Eisenhower

"Retiring is just practicing up to be dead. That doesn't take any practice."
Paul Harvey

"Whoever said money can't buy happiness simply didn't know where to go shopping."
Bo Derek

"The undecideds could vote one way or the other."
George H.W. Bush

"I'm too old to retire and too old to go back to work."
Barry Goldwater

"Farming looks mighty easy when your plow is a pencil and you're a thousand miles from the corn field."
Dwight Eisenhower

"It is a very lonely life that a man leads, who becomes aware of truths before their times."
Thomas Brackett Reed

"One of the lessons of history is that nothing is often a good thing to do and always a clever thing to say."
Will Durant

"If you want total security, go to prison. There you're fed, clothed, given medical care and so on. The only thing lacking – is freedom."
Dwight D. Eisenhower

"After about twenty years of marriage, I'm finally starting to scratch the surface of what women want and I think the answer lies somewhere between conversation and chocolate."
Mel Gibson

"I'm pretty sure there will be duck-hunting in heaven and I can't wait!"
Mike Huckabee

"The only summit meeting that can succeed is one that does not take place."
Barry Goldwater

"The system, if it is operating properly, is designed to save the President from himself."
Brent Scowcroft

"Politics is just like show business. You need a big opening. Then you coast for a while. Then you need a big finish."
Ronald Reagan

"What is the point of competing for a trophy if everyone gets a trophy?"
Glenn Beck

"If wrinkles must be written upon our brows, let them not be written upon the heart."
James Garfield

"The paths of glory lead but to the grave, but so do all other paths."
George Will

"One of the privileges of intellectuals is that they are free to be scandalously asinine without harming their reputation."
Eric Hoffer

"Success sometimes can really bite you in the shorts."
Donny Osmond

"If you want to get rid of pork in Washington, stop feeding the hogs."
George W. Bush

"Perhaps one of the most important accomplishments of my administration has been minding my own business."
Calvin Coolidge

"Washington is like Salem. If we're not lynching somebody twenty-four hours a day in this wretched town, we're not happy."
Tom Korologos

"A thief is more moral than a congressman; when a thief steals your money, he doesn't demand you thank him."
Walter E. Williams

"Even Albert Einstein reportedly needed help on his 1040 form."
Ronald Reagan

"Hollywood is a town that has to be seen to be disbelieved."
Walter Winchell

"CNN has gone to the dark side."
Bill O'Reilly

"The nice thing about being a celebrity is that when you bore people, they think it's their fault."
Henry Kissinger

"The only people who do not change their minds are incompetents in asylums, and those in cemeteries."
Everett Dirksen

"I did keep a grocery, and I did sell cotton, candles, and cigars, and sometimes whiskey. I remember in those days that Mr. Douglas was one of my best customers. Many a time have I stood on one side of the counter and sold whiskey to Mr. Douglas on the other side, but the difference between us now is this: I have left my side of the counter, but Mr. Douglas still sticks to his as tenaciously as ever."
Abraham Lincoln

"To be absolutely certain about something, one must know everything or nothing about it."
Henry A. Kissinger

"Creative semantics is the key to contemporary government; it consists of talking in strange tongues lest the public learn the inevitable inconveniently early."
George Will

"I had pro offers from the Detroit Lions and Green Bay Packers, who were pretty hard up for linemen in those days. If I had gone into professional football, the name Jerry Ford might have been a household word today."
Gerald Ford

"If Bill was all id, Hillary is all superego."
Rich Lowry

"We have a threefold responsibility to people – get them baptized, get them saved, and get them registered to vote."
Jerry Falwell

"Only two kinds of problems ever reach my desk; those marked urgent and those marked important – and I spend so much time on the urgent, I never get to the important."
Dwight Eisenhower

"What a joy it is to see really professional media manipulation."
William Safire

"Many people spend more time in planning the wedding than they do in planning the marriage."
Zig Ziglar

"Because of the pervasive bugging, I did not dictate any diary entries while we were in the Soviet Union. The Soviets were curiously unsubtle in this regard. A member of my staff reported having casually told his secretary that he would like an apple, and ten minutes later a maid came and put a bowl of apples on the table."
Richard Nixon

"Body piercing is a powerful, compelling visual statement that says: 'In today's competitive job market, what can I do to make myself less employable?'"
Dennis Miller

"I like to do my principal research in bars, where people are more likely to tell the truth or, at least, lie less convincingly than they do in briefings and books."
P.J. O'Rourke

"I thought it was extraordinary that Richard Nixon went on *Meet the Press* and spent an entire hour with Chris Wallace, Tom Brokaw, and John Chancellor. That should put an end to the talk that he hasn't been punished enough."
Ronald Reagan

"Ronald Reagan has a story for every occasion. Bill Clinton has an excuse."
Fred Barnes

"Public debt is paying for a dead horse. Private debt is buying a live one."
Herbert Hoover

"I bet you anything I could destroy Milton Friedman in a debate about economics – so long as the audience was comprised of five year olds."
Jonah Goldberg

"You can't shoot an idea."
Thomas Dewey

"A politician's words reveal less about what he thinks about his subject than what he thinks about his audience."
George Will

"The American people have respect for privacy on only two occasions: One of them is prayer and the other is fishing, and Presidents can't pray all the time."
Herbert Hoover

"I get my exercise acting as pallbearer to my friends who exercise."
Chauncey Depew

"I have a simple philosophy: Fill what's empty. Empty what's full. Scratch where it itches."
Alice Roosevelt Longworth

"If I could give people one piece of advice, it would be: 'Never go up to someone and say that you didn't vote for her husband.'"
Barbara Bush

"Collecting more taxes than is absolutely necessary is legalized robbery."
Calvin Coolidge

"There exists, we discover, a committee that will inform young draftable Americans how to beat the draft. Among the quaint suggestions being offered is that a draftee feign homosexuality. I expect some of those who would try this dodge could make pretty convincing demonstrations."
William F. Buckley, Jr.

"I've kind of fashioned my life after a Slinky. Bend me in a million shapes, and eventually I'll spring back to what I originally was."
Sylvester Stallone

"Fighting battles is like courting girls. Those who make the most pretensions and are boldest usually win."
Rutherford B. Hayes

"The other day, someone told me the difference between a democracy and a people's democracy. It's the same difference between a jacket and a straightjacket."
Ronald Reagan

"What's the difference between a hockey mom and a pit bull? Lipstick."
Sarah Palin

"Even in this room full of proud Manhattan democrats, I can't shake that feeling that some people here are pulling for me... I'm delighted to see you here tonight, Hillary."
John McCain

"Don't worry over what the newspapers say. I don't. Why should anyone else? I told the truth to the newspaper correspondents – but when you tell the truth to them, they are at sea."
William Howard Taft

"If John Kerry had a dollar for every time he bragged about serving in Vietnam -- oh wait, he does."
Ann Coulter

"Nolan Ryan is pitching much better now that he has his curve ball straightened out."
Joe Garagiola

"I would say that most of the scientists I've met in the biomedical sciences, if not controlled, would use human beings as guinea pigs."
Michael Savage

"A conservative is a person who comes to Bentonville, Arkansas, to study Wal-Mart and learn how to fix the post office. A liberal is a person who comes to Bentonville, Arkansas, to make Wal-Mart like the post office."
Newt Gingrich

"The President is alleged to have told Lewinsky that oral sex is not prohibited in the Bible and therefore is not adultery… It's an interesting pickup line."
Cal Thomas

"Peace may be the extension of war by other means."
Jeane Kirkpatrick

"I'm wrestling with two Japanese wrestlers three times a week. I am not the age or the build one would think to be whirled lightly over an opponent's head and batted down to the mattress without damage. But they're so skillful that I have not been hurt at all. My throat is a little sore, because once when one of them had me in a stranglehold, I also got hold of his windpipe and thought I could perhaps choke him off before he could choke me. However, he got ahead."
Theodore Roosevelt

"My doctors told me this morning my blood pressure is down so low that I can start reading the newspapers."
Ronald Reagan

"Tired mothers find that spanking takes less time than reasoning and penetrates sooner to the seat of the memory."
Will Durant

"Those who trust to chance must abide by the results of chance."
Calvin Coolidge

"We are not retreating – we are advancing in another direction."
Douglas MacArthur

"I have often been accused of putting my foot in my mouth, but I will never put my hands in your pocket."
Spiro Agnew

"Show me an elitist, and I'll show you a loser."
Tom Clancy

"I won't say the papers misquote me, but I sometimes wonder where Christianity would be today if some of those reporters had been Matthew, Mark, Luke, and John."
Barry Goldwater

"Neutrality where the Communists are concerned means three things: we get out; they stay in; they take over."
Richard Nixon

"On occasion, English has pursued other languages down alleyways to beat them unconscious and rifle their pockets for new vocabulary."
Booker T. Washington

"We recognize journalists have to kill somebody each week."
Roger Ailes

"It's no secret that I wear a hearing aid. Well, just the other day, all of a sudden, it went haywire. We discovered the KGB had put a listening device in my listening device."
Ronald Reagan

"I always say, as you know, that if my fellow citizens want to go to Hell I will help them. It's my job."
Oliver Wendell Holmes, Jr.

"I know no method to secure the repeal of bad or obnoxious laws so effective as their stringent execution."
Ulysses S. Grant

"One of the enduring truths of the nation's capital is that bureaucrats survive."
Gerald Ford

"If you're gonna be a failure, at least be one at something you enjoy."
Sylvester Stallone

"Actually, I do have a vision for the nation, and our goal is a simple one: By the time I leave office, I want every single American to be able to set the clock on his VCR."
George H.W. Bush

"If you don't know who you are before you get to Washington, D.C., this is a poor place to find out."
Alan Simpson

"There are only two reasons to sit in the back row of an airplane: Either you have diarrhea, or you're anxious to meet people who do."
Henry Kissinger

"I was first to break the news about the death of Lady Diana. The CNN team couldn't get into makeup fast enough."
Matt Drudge

"Education is learning what you didn't even know you didn't know."
Daniel J. Boorstin

"Look at me! I'm sweet and lovable!"
Donald Rumsfeld

"In the last 1,000 years, the Arabs have translated as many books as Spain translates in just one year."
Larry Elder

"The unemployment numbers are down to the lowest in twenty-five years... the principal credit goes to Janet Reno, who continues to appoint special prosecutors."
Dick Armey

"Nobody has milked one performance better than me – and I'm damned proud of it."
Bruce Jenner

"I can think of nothing more boring for the American public than to have to sit in their living rooms for a whole half hour looking at my face on their television screens."
Dwight Eisenhower

"Blessed is he who expects no gratitude, for he shall not be disappointed."
William Bennett

"Public office is the last refuge of a scoundrel."
Boies Penrose

"They have a right to work wherever they want to – as long as they have dinner ready when you get home."
John Wayne

"Calvinism was the child of indigestion."
Robert Green Ingersoll

"America is a well-watered country, and the inhabitants know all the fishing holes. The Americans also produce millions of automobiles. These coordinate forces of inalienable right, the automobile and the call of the fishing hole, propel the man and boy to a search of all the water within a radius of 150 miles at weekends alone. He extends it to a radius of 500 miles on his summer holidays. These radii of operations… greatly overlap. Not surprisingly, the time between bites has become longer and longer, and the fish have become wiser and wiser."
Herbert Hoover

"Even the best psychiatrist is like a blindfolded auto mechanic poking around under your hood with a giant foam 'We're #1' finger."
Dennis Miller

"Bill Clinton shares with the hummingbird the ability to turn 180 degrees in a split second."
Haley Barbour

"I'd give up golf if I didn't have so many sweaters."
Bob Hope

"They tell us that fuel-burning SUVs are bad for America, but flag-burning SOBs aren't."
Sean Hannity

"A government is not legitimate merely because it exists."
Jeane Kirkpatrick

"Anger management comes when they put me in the ground."
Michael Savage

"If you're hanging around with nothing to do and the zoo is closed, come over to the Senate. You'll get the same kind of feeling and you won't have to pay."
Bob Dole

"I can think of nothing less-pleasurable than a life devoted to pleasure."
John D. Rockefeller

"A free-speech clause without religion would be Hamlet without the prince."
Antonin Scalia

"Socialism in Great Britain accomplished little more than to freeze the capitalist economy at its point of least efficiency."
John Dos Passos

"There's only one place where inflation is made – that's in Washington."
Milton Friedman

"I'm more concerned about members of Congress being drug-free than I am about members of the Yankees or Giants."
Pat Sajak

"Before I took up my current line of work, I got to know a thing or two about negotiating when I represented the Screen Actors Guild in contract talks with the studios. After the studios, Gorbachev was a snap."
Ronald Reagan

"American diplomacy is easy on the brain, but hell on the feet."
Charles Dawes

"The three-martini lunch is the epitome of American efficiency. Where else can you get an earful, a bellyful, and a snootful at the same time?"
Gerald Ford

"More young people believe they'll see a U.F.O. than that they'll see their own Social Security benefits."
Mitch McConnell

"Baseball, it is said, is only a game. True. And the Grand Canyon is only a hole in Arizona. Not all holes, or games, are created equal."
George Will

"Whenever I hear anyone arguing for slavery, I feel a strong impulse to see it tried on him personally."
Abraham Lincoln

"Our blood will turn from red to blue, although our money is but new."
Walter Annenberg

"The sport of skiing consists of wearing three thousand dollars' worth of clothes and equipment and driving two hundred miles in the snow in order to stand around at a bar and get drunk."
P.J. O'Rourke

"To say nothing, especially when speaking, is half the art of diplomacy."
Will Durant

"Giving your book to Hollywood is like turning your daughter into a pimp."
Tom Clancy

"Clinton lied. A man might forget where he parks or where he lives, but he never forgets oral sex, no matter how bad it is."
Barbara Bush

"I worry incessantly that I might be too clear."
Alan Greenspan

"The President, with the enormous responsibility that he has, must not be constantly preening in front of a mirror. I don't worry about polls. I don't worry about image… I never have."
Richard Nixon

"If homosexuality was the normal way, God would have made Adam and Bruce."
Anita Bryant

"Siberia is never mild,
And never very nice.
They send a lot of people there,
And put them all on ice."
Jimmy Stewart

"I said to my liberal friend that we are fundamentally the same. I spend money like it's my money and you spend money like it's my money."
Dick Armey

"I will not make age an issue in this campaign. I am not going to exploit, for political purposes, my opponent's youth and inexperience."
Ronald Reagan

"The warning message we sent the Russians was a calculated ambiguity that would be clearly understood."
Alexander Haig

"A fact without a figure is a tragic final act, but one thing worse in this universe is a theory without a fact."
George Shultz

"ACLU and Jesus – they don't get along."
Glenn Beck

"The superpowers often behave like two heavily armed blind men feeling their way around a room, each believing himself in mortal peril from the other, whom he assumes to have perfect vision."
Henry Kissinger

"I can't speak for any other marriage, but the secret of our marriage is that we have absolutely nothing in common."
Mamie Eisenhower

"During a political campaign, everyone is concerned with what a candidate will do on this or that question if he is elected, except the candidate; he's too busy wondering what he'll do if he isn't elected."
Everett Dirksen

"I've learned to look like I'm listening to long confusing plots of cartoons and comic books when I'm actually sound asleep or making grocery shopping lists in my head."
Patricia Heaton

"You have to stand every day three or four hours of visitors. Nine-tenths of them want something they ought not to have. If you keep dead still, they will run down in three or four minutes. If you even cough or smile, they will start up all over again."
Calvin Coolidge

"I have the most reliable friend that you can have in American politics – ready money."
Phil Gramm

"Dan would rather play golf than have sex any day."
Marilyn Quayle

"Much of what Mr. Wallace calls his global thinking is, no matter how you slice it, still globaloney."
Clare Boothe Luce

"Las Vegas is really a wonderful place. Where else outside of government do people throw money away? The big difference, of course, is that here you can do it yourself; in government, we do it for you."
Ronald Reagan

"Like the Soviet economy, our public housing system is a morass of complicated regulations, perverse incentives, confused jurisdictional lines, and bureaucratic lethargy. But the worst part is that the system doesn't really work."
Alfonse D'Amato

"I got away with murder. I'm now more careful about what I say. Slightly."
Barbara Bush

"You can fool some of the people all of the time, and all of the people some of the time, but you cannot fool all of the people all the time."
Abraham Lincoln

"The truth will set you free, but first it will make you miserable."
James A. Garfield

"If you can't stand the heat, don't go to Cancun in the summer."
Ben Stein

"As long as there are only three to four people on the floor, the country is in good hands. It's only when you have fifty to sixty in the Senate that you want to be concerned."
Bob Dole

"Mule, thee knows that because of my religion I cannot beat thee, or curse thee, or abuse thee. But, mule, what thee doesn't know is that I can sell thee to an Episcopalian."
Dwight Eisenhower

"The real minimum wage is zero."
Thomas Sowell

"Our founders first defined that purpose here in Philadelphia. Ben Franklin was here. Thomas Jefferson. And, of course, George Washington – or, as his friends called him, 'George W.'"
George W. Bush

"We are showing a dismaying tendency to recast God in Man's image."
James L. Buckley

"The trick in eating crow is pretending it tastes good."
William Safire

"I've endured a great deal of ridicule without much malice, and have received a great deal of kindness not quite free from ridicule."
Abraham Lincoln

"It's no longer a question of staying healthy. It's a question of finding a sickness you like."
Jackie Mason

"I may be President of the United States, but my private life is nobody's damn business."
Chester Arthur

"In civilized societies, if you are offended by a cartoon, you do not burn flags, take up guns and raid buildings, chant death to your opponents, or threaten suicide bombings. You write a letter to the editor."
Michelle Malkin

"Votes are the professional politicians' idea of the food of Gods, which is kept in pork barrels."
Herbert Hoover

"Some critics complain that Gary Hart doesn't have any experience in foreign policy. But that's not true. Why, just yesterday he had breakfast at the International House of Pancakes."
George H.W. Bush

"Irony is an ill wind that bites the hand that feeds our fashionable cynicism."
Dan Quayle

"You can never underestimate the ability of the democrats to wet their finger and hold it to the wind."
Ronald Reagan

"Truth has never been timed to suit the tastes of the people who do not want to hear it. In view of the way the Preacher was treated, it would seem that the Sermon on the Mount was badly timed."
Herbert Hoover

"Treat each federal dollar as if it was hard earned; it was – by a taxpayer."
Donald Rumsfeld

"Feeling good about government is like looking on the bright side of any catastrophe. When you quit looking the bright side, the catastrophe is still there."
P.J. O'Rourke

"It's very easy to get advice and very hard to get consent."
Richard Nixon

"I'm not intolerant. I just know what it says in the Scriptures."
Jesse Helms

"The man who loves other countries as much as his own stands on a level with the man who loves other women as much as he loves his own wife."
Theodore Roosevelt

"Force is all-conquering, but its victories are short-lived."
Abraham Lincoln

"A good rule of thumb is if you've made it to thirty-five and your job still requires you to wear a name tag, you've probably made a serious vocational error."
Dennis Miller

"An Englishman who was wrecked on a strange shore and wandering along the coast came to a gallows with a victim hanging on it, and fell down to his knees and thanked God that he at last beheld a sign of civilization."
James Garfield

"It only takes one vote to win the vice presidential nomination."
Bob Dole

"A woman is like a teabag; you never know how strong she is until she gets in hot water."
Nancy Reagan

"The democrats are in a real bind. They won't get elected unless things get worse – and things won't get worse unless they're elected."
Jeane Kirkpatrick

"When I was on my way to the podium a gentleman stopped me and said I was as good a politician as I was an actor. What a cheap shot."
Arnold Schwarzenegger

"On last Sunday's *Meet the Press*, Gore showed that he has an enormous hole in his moral ozone layer."
Cal Thomas

"How do you tell a communist? Well, it's someone who reads Marx and Lenin. And how do you tell an anti-communist? It's someone who understands Marx and Lenin."
Ronald Reagan

"If you want a guarantee, buy a toaster."
Clint Eastwood

"People say I'm indecisive, but I don't know about that."
George H.W. Bush

"As far as Saddam Hussein being a great military strategist, he is neither a strategist, nor is he schooled in the operational art, nor is he a tactician, nor is he a general, nor is he a soldier. Other than that, he's a great military man."
Norman Schwarzkopf

"Since time immemorial man has heard no cry more agonized than that of the deposed bureaucrat or the demoted politician."
Dwight Eisenhower

"Some of us learn from other people's mistakes and the rest of us have to be other people."
Zig Ziglar

"I have come to the conclusion that the major part of the President is to increase the gate receipts of expositions and fairs and bring tourists into the town."
William Howard Taft

"You can discover what your enemy fears most by observing the means he uses to frighten you."
Eric Hoffer

"Democrats get totally preoccupied with things that voters don't care about."
Lee Atwater

"The trouble with socialism, a European observer once remarked, is socialism. The trouble with capitalism is capitalists."
William F. Buckley, Jr.

"You will discover that elder statesmen are little regarded by the opposition party until they get over eighty years of age and are harmless."
Herbert Hoover

"I can still remember the first time I ever heard Hubert Humphrey speak. He was in the second hour of a five minute talk."
Gerald Ford

"I know what it's like to pull the Republican lever for the first time, because I used to be a Democrat myself, and I can tell you it only hurts for a minute and then it feels just great."
Ronald Reagan

"My four years at Berkley represent two of the happiest weeks of my life."
Michael Medved

"One biscuit, with plenty of butter, is worth all the tracts ever distributed."
Robert Green Ingersoll

"If the Clintons' marriage were any more about convenience, they'd have to install a Slurpee machine and a Slim-Jim rack."
Dennis Miller

"What is conservative? Is it not adherence to the old and tried against the new and untried?"
Abraham Lincoln

"Even a paranoid has some real enemies."
Henry Kissinger

"Too many people expect wonders from democracy, when the most wonderful thing of all is just having it."
Walter Winchell

"A man is usually more careful of his money than of his principles."
Oliver Wendell Holmes, Jr.

"I want to be Robin to Bush's Batman."
Dan Quayle

"I have often said that the one thing worse for a politician than being wrong is being dull. But it is better to be dull than to be silly."
Richard Nixon

"I have one consolation. No one candidate was ever elected ex-President by such a large majority."
William Howard Taft

"If I've still got my pants on in the second scene, I think they've sent me the wrong script."
Mel Gibson

"Reports that say that something hasn't happened are always interesting to me, because as we know, there are known knowns; there are things we know we know. We also know there are known unknowns; that is to say we know there are some things we do not know. But there are also unknown unknowns – the ones we don't know we don't know."
Donald Rumsfeld

"I'm not arrogant. I just believe there's no human problem that couldn't be solved – if people would simply do as I tell 'em."
Don Regan

"When was the last time you bought a car – even a good cheese or videocassette recorder – and the label read: 'Made in the U.S.S.R.'?"
Ronald Reagan

"I'm afraid the country is not ready for a President who might have a tiger tattooed on his rear end."
George Shultz

"General Cass is a general of splendidly successful charges – charges, to be sure, not upon the public enemy, but upon the public treasury."
Abraham Lincoln

"We've had a Congress that's spent money like John Edwards at a beauty shop."
Mike Huckabee

"It is extraordinary how reluctant aged judges are to retire and to give up their accustomed work. They seem to be tenacious in the appearance of adequacy."
Charles Evans Hughes

"I invited all the conservatives in Massachusetts to come hear me today and I'm glad to report that they are both here."
Mitt Romney

"Many Americans don't like the simple things. That's what they have against conservatives."
Barry Goldwater

"If you're a liberal, anything you say is protected. If you're a conservative, anything you say is hateful."
Laura Schlessinger

"I was often seasick, but that semi-comatose condition has its advantages. It makes one oblivious to danger."
Herbert Hoover

"Liberalism is totalitarianism with a human face."
Thomas Sowell

"If there is a 50-50 chance that something can go wrong, then nine times out of ten it will."
Paul Harvey

"Christmas begins about the first of December with an office party and ends when you finally realize what you spent, around April fifteenth of the next year."
P.J. O'Rourke

"When the people are waving at you, wave your arms and move your lips, so you look like you're talking to them."
Dwight Eisenhower

"It is only a matter of time before someone burns a flag, calls it 'kinetic art', and gets a great grant to take his act on the road."
George Will

"Man cannot live by bread alone; he must have peanut butter."
James A. Garfield

"England is the only country where food is more dangerous than sex."
Jackie Mason

"I do not know whether it is prejudice or not, but I always have a very high opinion of a state whose chief product is corn."
Benjamin Harrison

"They say women talk too much. If you have worked in Congress you know that the filibuster was invented by men."
Clare Boothe Luce

"The best part about being Vice President is presiding over the Senate. Where else could I have Barry Goldwater addressing me as Mr. President?"
Nelson Rockefeller

"I'm not a hawk. I'm a dove – a heavily armed dove."
Jack Kemp

"Balancing the budget is a little like protecting your virtue: You just have to learn to say no."
Ronald Reagan

"I always figured the American public wanted a solemn ass for President, so I went along with them."
Calvin Coolidge

"Truce is an old Arabic word. Goes way, way back in Islamic-Arabic culture, and it means: 'We will get you later.'"
Rush Limbaugh

"My dog Millie knows more about foreign affairs than those two bozos."
George H.W. Bush

"I always turn to the sports pages first, which records people's accomplishments. The front page has nothing but man's failures."
Earl Warren

"They told me to go for the jugular – so I did. It was mine."
Bob Dole

"You could mention my name in any hallway in any academic institution and you would have people foaming at the mouth."
David Horowitz

"Anyone who eats pork rinds can't be all good."
Barbara Bush

"I bring out the worst in my enemies and that's how I get them to defeat themselves."
Roy Cohn

"A gentleman told me recently he doubted if I would vote for the angel Gabriel if he was found at the head of the Democratic Party, to which I responded that the angel Gabriel would never be found in such company."
Theodore Roosevelt

"Presidential ambition is a disease that can only be cured by embalming fluid."
John McCain

"As people do better, they start voting like republicans – unless they have too much education and vote democratic, which proves there can be too much of a good thing."
Karl Rove

"You can't eat awards – nor, more to the point, drink 'em."
John Wayne

"I never wanted to get out of a place as much as I did to get out of the presidency."
Ulysses S. Grant

"If Al Gore winds up losing this election, I understand Tony Robbins is going to hire him as a motivational speaker. His topic: 'How to almost win.'"
Cal Thomas

"You know you've reached middle age when your weightlifting consists merely of standing up."
Bob Hope

"There are three kinds of pollution today – real, hysterical, and political."
Ronald Reagan

"I prayed for twenty years but received no answer until I prayed with my legs."
Frederick Douglass

"She's been on more laps than a napkin."
Walter Winchell

"The absence of alternatives clears the mind marvelously."
Henry Kissinger

"It's about time law enforcement got as organized as organized crime."
Rudy Giuliani

"I'd rather be on the sports page than on the front page."
Gerald Ford

"Mr. Gore Vidal, the playwright and quipster who lost a Congressional race a few years ago but continues to seek out opportunities to advertise his ignorance of contemporary affairs."
William F. Buckley, Jr.

"The ballot is stronger than the bullet."
Abraham Lincoln

"You do not lead by hitting people over the head – that's assault, not leadership."
Dwight Eisenhower

"You could put on monkeys jumping up and down and get bigger numbers than MSNBC."
Bill O'Reilly

"You don't win campaigns with a diet of dishwater and milk toast."
Richard Nixon

"Ladies and gentlemen, I feel chipper tonight. I survived the White House shake-up."
George W. Bush

"If I've told you once, I've told you a thousand times – resist hyperbole."
William Safire

"It has been my experience that folks who have no vices have very few virtues."
Abraham Lincoln

"A revered President long since dead once told me that there was no solution to this relation of the White House to the press; that there would never be a President who could satisfy the press until he was twenty years dead."
Herbert Hoover

"The trees in Siberia are miles apart – that's why the dogs are so fast."
Bob Hope

"If Thomas Edison were a kid today, I doubt we'd have the light bulb."
Michael Savage

"They say hard work never hurt anybody, but I figure why take the chance."
Ronald Reagan

"A few months ago Kennedy's mother said: 'You have a choice. Do you want to go to camp this year or run for president?'"
Bob Hope

"A man over ninety is a great comfort to all his elderly neighbors; he is a picket-guard at the extreme outpost; and the young folks of sixty and seventy feel that the enemy must get by him before he can come near their camp."
Oliver Wendell Holmes, Jr.

"Everybody's business is nobody's business, and nobody's business is my business."
Clara Barton quote

"George is not a good quarreler – he doesn't like to quarrel, he likes to discuss."
Barbara Bush

"There is an obvious cure for failure – and that is success. But what is the cure for success?"
Daniel J. Boorstin

"Being a star is an agent's dream, not an actor's."
Robert Duvall

"All free governments are managed by the combined wisdom and folly of the people."
James Garfield

"Victory goes to the player who makes the next-to-last mistake."
Jackie Mason

"Whatever it is that the government does, sensible Americans would prefer that the government does it to somebody else. This is the idea behind foreign policy."
P.J. O'Rourke

"What kills a skunk is the publicity it gives itself."
Abraham Lincoln

"Ultra-Liberal: Term not used; one presumably cannot be too liberal. I read six newspapers and countless journals. I have almost never encountered the term 'ultra-liberal' or 'arch-liberal', yet often read about 'ultra-conservatives' and 'arch-conservatives.'"
Dennis Prager

"I kind of like ducking questions."
George W. Bush

"And the ultimate thing is, I may not be the expert that some people are on foreign policy, but I did stay in a Holiday Inn Express last night."
Mike Huckabee

"The mind is like the stomach. It is not how much you put into it that counts, but how much it digests."
Albert Jay Nock

"You know all those Secret Service men you've seen around me? When I play golf, they get combat pay."
Gerald Ford

"Saying the Washington Post is just a newspaper is like saying Rasputin was just a country priest."
Patrick Buchanan

"Government is like a baby – an alimentary canal with a big appetite at one end and no sense of responsibility at the other."
Ronald Reagan

"I can promise you that when I go to Sacramento, I will pump up Sacramento!"
Arnold Schwarzenegger

"The puppies are sleeping on the Washington Post and New York Times. It's the first time in history these papers have been used to prevent leaks."
George H.W. Bush

"If you don't drive your business, you will be driven out of business."
B.C. Forbes

"A page of history is worth a volume of logic."
Oliver Wendell Holmes, Jr.

"I have a very strict gun control policy – if there's a gun around, I want to be in control of it."
Clint Eastwood

"We are suffering today more from frozen confidence than we are from frozen securities."
Herbert Hoover

"No matter what you do, be honest. That stands out in Washington."
Barry Goldwater

"If Robert Byrd were your grandfather and he came to Thanksgiving dinner and went off on one of these demented screeds, everybody would sit there smiling at him, and as soon as he left the room, somebody'd say: 'Hey, what the hell are we gonna do about grandpa?'"
Dennis Miller

"How has retirement affected my golf game? A lot more people beat me now."
Dwight Eisenhower

"I understand my critics are fixated and pathologically disoriented, but they are my opponents. Why would I try to correct them?"
Newt Gingrich

"Statistics are like alienists – they will testify for either side."
Fiorello La Guardia

"A man who has never gone to school may steal from a freight car, but if he has a university education, he may steal the whole railroad."
Theodore Roosevelt

"Playing polo is like trying to play golf during an earthquake."
Sylvester Stallone

"The capacity to admire others is not my most fully developed trait."
Henry Kissinger

"Autobiography is mostly alibiography."
Clare Boothe Luce

"By the time you reach my age, you've made plenty of mistakes if you've lived your life properly."
Ronald Reagan

"Businessmen want their companies to be as big as possible. Bureaucrats want their bureaucracies to be as big as possible. And Ted Kennedy wants his tumbler to be as big as possible."
Laura Ingraham

"I may not know enough about being President, but I do know that a lot of decisions can be made on golf courses."
Warren Harding

"I am probably the only mom in America who knows exactly what her son is doing and where he is doing it."
Barbara Bush

"I feel terrible for all the mothers in the state of Arizona. Because, as you know, Barry Goldwater from Arizona ran for President of the United States, Morris Udall from Arizona ran for President of the United States, Bruce Babbitt from Arizona ran for President of the United States, and I, John McCain from Arizona ran for President of the United States. Arizona may be the only state in the nation where mothers no longer tell their children that some day they can grow up and be President of the United States."
John McCain

"If $120,000 a year is the best job you ever had, you haven't really done very much."
Tom Clancy

"I have been told I was on the road to hell, but I had no idea it was just a mile down the road with a dome on it."
Abraham Lincoln

"The three major administrative problems on a campus are sex for the students, athletics for the alumni, and parking for the faculty."
Robert M. Hutchins

"If Washington is a two-party town, why can't Hollywood be one too?"
Jon Voight

"Lawyers spend a great deal of their time shoveling smoke."
Oliver Wendell Holmes, Jr.

"The United Nations was not set up to be a reformatory. It was assumed that you would be good before you got in and not that being in would make you good."
John Foster Dulles

"I would leave the country if I were President."
Sylvester Stallone

"People who've had a hanging in the family don't like to talk about a rope."
Calvin Coolidge

"It either is or ought to be evident to everyone that business has to prosper before anybody can get any benefit from it."
Theodore Roosevelt

"People are always asking me if there are any politicians in Washington with convictions. Yes, I tell them. They're all in federal prison."
Cal Thomas

"If you like laws and sausages, you should never watch either one being made."
Ronald Reagan

"Supporting the Equal Rights Amendment is like trying to kill a fly with a sledge hammer. You don't kill the fly, but you end up breaking the furniture."
Phyllis Schlafly

"If anyone tells you that America's best days are behind her, they're looking the wrong way."
George H.W. Bush

"In case you missed it, a few days ago Senator Clinton tried to spend $1 million on the Woodstock Concert Museum. Now, ladies and gentlemen, I wasn't there. I'm sure it was a cultural and pharmaceutical event. I was tied up at the time."
John McCain

"If I could paraphrase a well-know statement by Will Rogers that he never met a man he didn't like – I'm afraid we have some people around here who have never met a tax they didn't hike."
Ronald Reagan

"Talking is more tiring than I thought."
Newt Gingrich

"If you see ten troubles coming down the road, you can be sure that nine will run into the ditch before they reach you."
Calvin Coolidge

"It will cost me some struggle to keep from despising the office seeker."
James Garfield

"Woe to him inside a nonconformist clique who does not conform with nonconformity."
Eric Hoffer

"Take the two leading liberal columnists at the New York Times, Maureen Dowd and Paul Krugman. As we all know, one's a whining self-parody of a hysterical liberal who lets feminine emotion and fear defeat reason and fact in almost every column. The other used to date Michael Douglas."
Jonah Goldberg

"Listening to democrats complain about inflation is like listening to germs complain about disease."
Spiro Agnew

"A pessimist is a man who thinks all women are bad. An optimist is a man who hopes they are."
Chauncey Depew

"The Iraqi forces are conducting the Mother of all Retreats."
Dick Cheney

"You can't know too much, but you can say too much."
Calvin Coolidge

"A woman who demands further gun control legislation is like a chicken who roots for Colonel Sanders."
Larry Elder

"Richard Nixon was just offered two million dollars by Schick to do a commercial – for Gillette."
Gerald Ford

"I always thought music was more important than sex. Then I thought – if I don't hear a concert for a year and a half it doesn't bother me."
Jackie Mason

"Politicians were talking themselves red, white, and blue in the face."
Clare Boothe Luce

"If you have a job without aggravations, you don't have a job."
Malcolm Forbes

"God is a Republican and Santa Claus is a Democrat."
P.J. O'Rourke

"Politics is not a bad profession. If you succeed, there are many rewards; if you disgrace yourself, you can always write a book."
Ronald Reagan

"It seems to be the profession of a President simply to hear other people talk."
William Howard Taft

"The reason Sumner doesn't believe in the Bible is because he didn't write it himself."
Ulysses S. Grant

"There will be good moments, and there will be less good moments."
Donald Rumsfeld

"When you're leading, don't talk."
Thomas Dewey

"What is a moderate interpretation of the text? Halfway between what it really means and what you'd like it to mean?"
Antonin Scalia

"The voters of Oregon have spoken, and I like the sound of their voices."
Richard Nixon

"New Hampshire is all retail politics. Make sure you shake every voter's hand twice."
John Sununu

"The shepherd drives the wolf from the sheep's throat, for which the sheep thanks the shepherd as his liberator, while the wolf denounces him for the same act... Plainly the sheep and the wolf are not agreed upon a definition of liberty."
Abraham Lincoln

"I wish I'd married a plumber. At least he'd be home by five o'clock."
Betty Ford

"The judgments that liberals render on public issues, domestic and foreign, are as predictable as the salivation of Pavlovian dogs."
James Burnham

"Optimist: A man who gets treed by a lion but enjoys the scenery."
Walter Winchell

"People often say that motivation doesn't last. Well, neither does bathing – that's why we recommend it daily."
Zig Ziglar

"When political action committees give money, they expect something in return other than good government."
Bob Dole

"We clamor for equality chiefly in matters in which we ourselves cannot hope to obtain excellence."
Eric Hoffer

"Subjecting the failure of twentieth century American liberalism to close analysis would be breaking a butterfly upon the wheel."
Russell Kirk

"In the United States today, we have more than our share of the nattering nabobs of negativism."
Spiro Agnew

"I let football and other extracurricular activities eat into my study time with the result that my grade average was closer to the C level required for eligibility than it was to straight A's. And even now I wonder what I might have accomplished if I'd studied harder."
Ronald Reagan

"A woman is the only thing I am afraid of that I know will not hurt me."
Abraham Lincoln

"To those of you who received honors, awards, and distinctions, I say well done. And to the C students, I say you, too, can be President of the United States."
George W. Bush

"Put not your trust in money, but put your money in trust."
Oliver Wendell Holmes, Jr.

"The Positive Woman spends her time, ingenuity, and efforts seizing her opportunities – not whining about past injustices."
Phyllis Schlafly

"I do benefits for all religions: I'd hate to blow the after-life on a technicality."
Bob Hope

"World War II was the last government program that really worked."
George Will

"The oilcan is mightier than the sword."
Everett Dirksen

"The White Sox are rightly called the 'Hitless Wonders' – their idea of offense is a walk, an error, and a hurricane."
Joe Garagiola

"Plato, Aristotle, and Shakespeare have been replaced by contemporary liberal works such as *Heather Has Two Mommies*, *Daddy's Roommate*, and Al Gore's *Earth in the Balance*."
Michael Savage

"The death penalty is one hundred percent effective in preventing recidivism."
George Will

"We have long since discovered that nothing lasts longer than a temporary government program."
Ronald Reagan

"There doesn't seem to be anything else for an ex-President to do but go into the country and raise big pumpkins."
Chester Arthur

"I was so self-conscious, every time football players went into a huddle, I thought they were talking about me."
Jackie Mason

"Fluency in the English language is something I'm often not accused of."
George H.W. Bush

"In the elaborate wardrobe of human emotions, guilt is the itchy wool turtleneck that's three sizes too small."
Dennis Miller

"Our intent will not be to create gridlock. Oh, except maybe from time to time."
Bob Dole

"I don't know who my grandfather was. I am much more concerned to know what his grandson will be."
Abraham Lincoln

"I tried being reasonable. I didn't like it."
Clint Eastwood

"Football is a mistake. It combines two of the worst things about American life. It is violence punctuated by committee meetings."
George Will

"The income tax has created more criminals than any other single act of government."
Barry Goldwater

"I just want to remind you that every vote counts. Vote early, and then vote often. That's what we do in Texas."
Barbara Bush

"I'm strictly a no-deal man."
Dwight Eisenhower

"I was told that people did not like negative ads. So I didn't run any. I lost."
Bob Dole

"A vote is like a rifle – its usefulness depends upon the character of the user."
Theodore Roosevelt

"Mr. Hitchcock did not say actors are cattle. He said they should be treated like cattle."
Jimmy Stewart

"My father taught me to work; he did not teach me to love it."
Abraham Lincoln

"We might as well address the patients in the lunatic asylum on finance, as to hope to change the tone of the House at present."
James Garfield

"The only true democracy in the world is experienced when a man is fishing – all men are equal before fishes."
Herbert Hoover

"The French are masters of 'the dog ate my homework' school of diplomatic relations."
P.J. O'Rourke

"No man ever listened himself out of a job."
Calvin Coolidge

"Whoever thought a tiny candy bar should be called 'fun size' was a moron."
Glenn Beck

"They kill good trees to put out bad newspapers."
James G. Watt

"What counts is not necessarily the size of the dog in the fight – it's the size of the fight in the dog."
Dwight Eisenhower

"In westerns you were permitted to kiss your horse, but never your girl."
Gary Cooper

"No people is wholly civilized where the distinction is drawn between stealing an office and stealing a purse."
Theodore Roosevelt

"Today's gossip is tomorrow's headlines."
Walter Winchell

"When politicians tell us the budget has been cut to the bone, they have barely sliced through the skin of the overweight sow known as the federal government."
Cal Thomas

"I'm sorry that some of the chairs on the left seem to be uncomfortable."
Ronald Reagan

"Your Majesty, I took the liberty because I was so desirous of visiting alone with you for a few minutes before the rest of the other peasants arrived."
Walter Annenberg

"Six imams removed from a US Airways flight from Minneapolis to Phoenix are calling on Muslims to boycott the airline. If only we could get Muslims to boycott all airlines, we could dispense with airport security altogether."
Ann Coulter

"When your outgo exceeds your income, the upshot may be your downfall."
Paul Harvey

"There is no such thing as a free lunch."
Milton Friedman

"Take all your dukes and marquesses and earls and viscounts, pack them into one chamber, call it the House of Lords to satisfy their pride and then strip it of all political power. It's a solution so perfectly elegant and preposterous that only the British could have managed it."
Charles Krauthammer

"Books serve to show a man that those original thoughts of his aren't very new after all."
Abraham Lincoln

"Rudeness is the weak man's imitation of strength."
Eric Hoffer

"Don't be 'consistent', but be simply true."
Oliver Wendell Holmes, Jr.

"Did the Pilgrims need subsidies?"
William E. Simon

"There is about as much danger of the establishment of religion in this country as there is of the return of sanity to the Supreme Court."
William F. Buckley, Jr.

"One of the reasons for retiring from public life was to avoid further speechmaking."
Calvin Coolidge

"If Thomas Edison had invented the electric light in the age of the welfare state, the democrats would immediately introduce a bill to protect the candle-making industry."
Newt Gingrich

"You better watch out. The common man is standing up and some day he's going to elect a policeman President of the United States."
Eric Hoffer

"The last stage of sentimentalism is homicidal mania."
Irving Babbitt

"It is very disappointing and hurtful. How come nobody ever thought that I had an affair with anyone?"
Barbara Bush

"Magazine buyers are easier to pick up than the book buyers."
Michael Savage

"Nothing is really real unless is happens on television."
Daniel Boorstin

"Never get into a wrestling match with a pig. You both get dirty, and the pig likes it."
John McCain

"Hope is the only bee that makes honey without flowers."
Robert Green Ingersoll

"It is a paradox that every dictator has climbed to power on the ladder of free speech. Immediately on attaining power each dictator has suppressed all free speech except his own."
Herbert Hoover

"It is said that the titles of most bills in Congress are like the titles of Marx Brothers movies (*Duck Soup*, *Animal Crackers*): they do not tell much about the contents."
George Will

"The quarterback's spending so much time behind the center that he may jeopardize his right to lead a Boy Scout troop."
Dennis Miller

"I was born at night, but it wasn't last night."
Haley Barbour

"If you watch a game, it's fun. If you play it, it's recreation. If you work at it, it's golf."
Bob Hope

"The White House is the leakiest place I've ever been in."
Ronald Reagan

"Plastic surgery is like a big elephant sitting in the Hollywood living room."
Patricia Heaton

"To me, the best candidate of all would be an astronaut. He can say: 'I was floating in outer space the whole time.'"
Frank Luntz

"Woe to him who teaches men faster than they can learn."
Will Durant

"It's my honor to speak to you as the leader of your country. And the great thing about America is you don't have to listen unless you want to."
George W. Bush

"Because brickbats can be used for murder, we do not need to stop building houses."
Herbert Hoover

"An idiot is no smarter if a billion people agree with him and a genius is no dumber if a billion people don't."
Jonah Goldberg

"I feel like a mosquito in a nudist colony. The real question is where to strike first."
Phil Gramm

"I love Thanksgiving turkey… it's the only time in Los Angeles that you see natural breasts."
Arnold Schwarzenegger

"There's a new fashion sweeping the country – skirts are shorter, pants are tighter, and the LBJ coattails are going out of style."
Richard Nixon

"Police in Washington D.C. are now using cameras to catch drivers who go through red lights. Many congressmen this week opposed the use of the red light cameras incorrectly assuming they were being used for surveillance at local brothels."
Dennis Miller

"You can lead the House to order, but you can't make it think."
William Weld

"If you think health care is expensive now, wait until you see what it costs when it's free."
P.J. O'Rourke

"If the twelve apostles were to be chosen nowadays, the interest of locality would have to be heeded."
Abraham Lincoln

"The conventional army loses if it does not win. The guerrilla wins if he does not lose."
Henry Kissinger

"Pale yellow ties became the insignia of the worker bees of the business world."
Tom Wolfe

"The only experience you gain in politics is how to be political."
Ronald Reagan

"I love flying. I've been to almost as many places as my luggage."
Bob Hope

"I do not suggest that you should not have an open mind, particularly as you approach college. But, don't keep your mind so open that your brains fall out."
William Bennett

"I am for lifting everyone off the social bottom. In fact, I am for doing away with the social bottom altogether."
Clare Boothe Luce

"Back in the thirties we were told we must collectivize the nation because the people were so poor. Now we are told we must collectivize the nation because the people are so rich."
William F. Buckley, Jr.

"I wish some of you would tell me the brand of whiskey that Grant drinks. I would like to send a barrel of it to my other generals."
Abraham Lincoln

"Governor Clinton's economic plan looks to me like 'broccoli economics'. He makes it sound good, but I find it hard to swallow."
George H.W. Bush

"Socialism in general has a record of failure so blatant that only an intellectual could ignore or evade it."
Thomas Sowell

"A balanced budget in itself is not a sacred word, but on the other hand it is not a bad word."
Dwight Eisenhower

"A best-seller was a book which somehow sold well because it was selling well."
Daniel J. Boorstin

"Name one area where the federal government visits and eventually does not take up permanent residence."
Cal Thomas

"Unlike the President, I inhaled. And then I threw up."
Christine Todd Whitman

"Study hard. There's no such thing as knowing too much. After all, you all want to grow up and be on *Who Wants to Be a Millionaire*, don't you?"
Barbara Bush

"Perhaps no emotion cools sooner than that of gratitude."
Benjamin Harrison

"We can't do everything at once, but we can do something at once."
Calvin Coolidge

"An expert is someone who is capable of articulating the interests of people with power."
Henry Kissinger

"Republicans believe every day is the Fourth of July, but democrats believe every day is April 15."
Ronald Reagan

"You know you're out of power when your limousine is yellow and your driver speaks Farsi."
James Baker

"We are struggling with a fantastic nightmare whose other name is Federal Bureaucracy."
Herbert Hoover

"Athletic proficiency is a mighty good servant, and like so many other good servants, a might bad master."
Theodore Roosevelt

"What's wrong with being a boring kind of guy?"
George H.W. Bush

"I was freezing in that loincloth."
James Caviezel

"Today's hard liner on law and order is yesterday's liberal who was mugged last night."
Ronald Reagan

"Once the toothpaste is out of the tube, it's hard to get back in."
H.R. Haldeman

"You can get a happy quotation anywhere if you have the eye."
Oliver Wendell Holmes, Jr.

"Better to remain silent and be thought a fool than to speak out and remove all doubt."
Abraham Lincoln

"Winning is like shaving – you do it every day or you wind up looking like a bum."
Jack Kemp

"I myself do not own a gun. I'm afraid of them. I'm too afraid I'd shoot the wrong person."
Barbara Bush

"Socialism has long since been discredited intellectually. But when did it get so creepy?"
William F. Buckley, Jr.

"I don't have any focus groups on talent and programming. If I need five people in a mall to be paid $40 to tell me how to do my job, I shouldn't do my job."
Roger Ailes

"The best view of big government is in the rear view mirror as you're driving away from it."
Ronald Reagan

"If Edwards gained sixty pounds and lost all his hair, he'd look like Dick Cheney!"
Neil Cavuto

"You can fool some of the people all the time, and those are the ones you want to concentrate on."
George W. Bush

"Reading about one's failings in the daily papers is one of the privileges of high office in this free country of ours."
Nelson Rockefeller

"I would just like to be mayor of Galena long enough to build a sidewalk from my house to the station."
Ulysses S. Grant

"The Soviet Union would remain a one-party nation even if an opposition party were permitted – because everyone would join that party."
Ronald Reagan

"The first twenty stories written about a public figure set the tone for the next two thousand and it is almost impossible to reverse it."
Charles Colson

"No TV performance takes such careful preparation as an off-the-cuff talk."
Richard Nixon

"Fiscal problems do a lot for moral uplift because sin takes a terrific shellacking from sin taxes."
George Will

"Ronald Reagan doesn't dye his hair – he's just prematurely orange."
Gerald Ford

"We shall sooner have the bird by hatching the egg than by smashing it."
Abraham Lincoln

"Seriousness is stupidity sent to college."
P.J. O'Rourke

"You know the difference between a lawyer and a catfish? One is a scum-sucking bottom-dweller. The other is a fish."
John McCain

"Sometimes our right hand doesn't know what our far-right hand is doing."
Ronald Reagan

"It's our borders, stupid."
Michael Savage

"I believe if we introduced the Lord's Prayer here, senators would propose a large number of amendments to it."
Henry Wilson

"Historic continuity with the past is not a duty, it is only a necessity."
Oliver Wendell Holmes, Jr.

"The reason Congress hasn't balanced the budget is that the sky hasn't fallen lately."
William Frenzel

"I feel like the fellow in jail who is watching his scaffold being built."
Dwight Eisenhower

"Anyone who says businessmen deal in facts, not fiction, has never read old five-year projections."
Malcolm Forbes

"Euphemisms for restricting trade are created by those who benefit from restrictions."
Dick Armey

"Why is it there are so many more horses' asses than there are horses?"
G. Gordon Liddy

"I want to see you shoot the way you shout."
Theodore Roosevelt

"We sometimes forget that until 1969, it was actually quite difficult to obtain a divorce in America. That all began to change after California passed its Family Law Act of 1969. Before that act, Californians could only be divorced for the following reasons – adultery, extreme cruelty, willful desertion, willful neglect, habitual intemperance, conviction of a felony, and incurable insanity. In other words, someone came out of the divorce looking really bad."
Laura Ingraham

"You don't need to be straight to die for your country. You just need to shoot straight."
Barry Goldwater

"I've been getting some flak about ordering the production of the B-1. How did I know it was an airplane? I thought it was a vitamin for the troops."
Ronald Reagan

"Professor Galbraith is horrified by the number of Americans who have bought cars with tail fins on them, and I am horrified by the number of Americans who take seriously the proposals of Mr. Galbraith."
William F. Buckley, Jr.

"A jury too frequently has at least one member more ready to hang the panel than to hang the traitor."
Abraham Lincoln

"After spending a year in Washington, I long for the realism and sensitivity of Hollywood."
Fred Thompson

"Dan Rather said that 'Castro feels a very deep and abiding connection' to the Cuban people. Maybe that's why he has so many of them in prison and in graves, so he will always have them close by."
Cal Thomas

"Nothing is easier than spending public money. It does not appear to belong to anybody. The temptation is overwhelming to bestow it on somebody."
Calvin Coolidge

"It's the gray-haired ladies who come and say: 'Gee, you look exactly like my mother!' that worries me a bit."
Barbara Bush

"If you're not in the Washington Post every day, you might as well not exist."
Newt Gingrich

"The buck stops with the guy who signs the checks."
Rupert Murdoch

"Going to college offered me the chance to play football for four more years."
Ronald Reagan

"My No. 1 goal is to not go to jail."
Michele Bachmann

"We are now in the Me Decade – seeing the upward roll of the third great religious wave in American history."
Tom Wolfe

"Remember the words of Chairman Mao: 'It's always darkest before it's totally black.'"
John McCain

"Like every well-trained Ohio man, I always had my plate the right side up when offices were falling."
William Howard Taft

"Mediocrity requires aloofness to preserve its dignity."
Charles G. Dawes

"Fewer people are bent from hard work than are crooked from avoiding it."
Zig Ziglar

"When the voters speak, I listen. Especially when the voter is saying someone else's name."
Phil Gramm

"If Thomas Jefferson thought taxation without representation was bad, he should see how it is with representation."
Rush Limbaugh

"If we do not succeed, then we run the risk of failure."
Dan Quayle

"Nothing conduces to brevity like a caving in of the knees."
Oliver Wendell Holmes, Jr.

"A liberal is one who says it's all right for an eighteen-year-old girl to perform in a pornographic movie as long as she gets paid minimum wage."
Irving Kristol

"You've seen one slum and you've seen them all."
Spiro Agnew

"A pundit is an expert on nothing but an authority on everything."
William Safire

"The search for a scapegoat is the easiest of all hunting expeditions."
Dwight Eisenhower

"If thirteen is a dangerous number, twenty-six ought to be twice as dangerous, and fifty-two, four times as terrible."
Robert Green Ingersoll

"Life is tough, but it's tougher when you're stupid."
John Wayne

"Governments tend not to solve problems, only rearrange them."
Ronald Reagan

"A gentleman will not insult me, and no man not a gentleman can insult me."
Frederick Douglass

"Conservatives divide the world in terms of good and evil while liberals do it in terms of the rich and poor."
Dennis Prager

"If you don't know where you are going, every road will get you nowhere."
Henry Kissinger

"Three-fifths to two-thirds of the federal budget consists of taking property from one American and giving it to another. Were a private person to do the same thing, we'd call it theft. When government does it, we euphemistically call it income redistribution, but that's exactly what thieves do – redistribute income."
Walter E. Williams

"I would like to take you seriously, but to do so would affront your intelligence."
William F. Buckley, Jr.

"I suffer from Truth in Mouth Syndrome."
Michael Savage

"Since I came to the White House I got two hearing aids, a colon operation, skin cancer, and a prostate operation – and I was shot. The damn thing is, I've never felt better in my life."
Ronald Reagan

"If I'm alive, what am I doing here? And if I'm dead, why do I have to go to the bathroom?"
Thomas Dewey

"I give special consideration to everybody."
Alfonse D'Amato

"We had a good year, except for Watergate."
Ron Ziegler

"We've finally given liberals a war against fundamentalism, and they don't want to fight it. They would, except it would put them on the same side as the United States."
Ann Coulter

"A former congressman once told me that 'any press is good press'. He'd clearly never seen my press."
Newt Gingrich

"Talleyrand once said to the first Napoleon that 'the United States is a giant without bones'. Since that time our gristle has been rapidly hardening."
James Garfield

"I didn't say I didn't say it. I said I didn't say I said it. I want to make that very clear."
George Romney

"Anyone who isn't thoroughly confused isn't thinking clearly."
Clare Boothe Luce

"Better give your path to a dog than be bitten by him in contesting for the right."
Abraham Lincoln

"I do not believe that any political campaign justifies the declaration of a moratorium on common sense."
Dwight Eisenhower

"If I take care of my character, my reputation will take care of itself."
Dwight Moody

"Most television has become like cigarettes. The content is so poisonous that labeling the product does nothing to help those who are irresponsible enough to ingest it."
Cal Thomas

"It's a very good question, very direct, and I'm not going to answer it."
George H. W. Bush

"The gold medal that was won last night by American Lindsey Vonn has been stripped. It was determined that President Obama has been going downhill faster than she has."
Mitt Romney

"Lending arms is like lending chewing gum. You don't get it back."
Robert Taft

"There cannot be a crisis next week. My schedule is already full."
Henry Kissinger

"My father was a Methodist, my mother was a Quaker. They got married and compromised and my father became a Quaker, too."
Richard Nixon

"I took the Canal Zone and let Congress debate, and while the debate goes on, the canal does, too."
Theodore Roosevelt

"At home, our enemy is no longer Red Coats, but red ink."
Ronald Reagan

"Oh, Lord. I didn't mean to say anything quotable."
Donald Rumsfeld

List of Speakers

Spiro Agnew
George Aiken
Roger Ailes
Walter Annenberg
Dick Armey
Chester Arthur
Lee Atwater
Irving Babbitt
Michele Bachmann
James Baker
Haley Barbour
Fred Barnes
Clara Barton
Glenn Beck
William Bennett
Shirley Temple Black
Jay Blossman
Daniel J. Boorstin
Rich Bond
Sonny Bono
Robert Bork
Clarence Brown
Anita Bryant
Patrick Buchanan
James L. Buckley
William F. Buckley, Jr.
James Burnham
Barbara Bush
George H.W. Bush
George W. Bush
Simon Cameron
Joseph Cannon
James Caviezel
Neil Cavuto
Mona Charen
Linda Chavez
Dick Cheney

Lynne Cheney
Tom Clancy
Roy Cohn
Charles Colson
John Connally
Calvin Coolidge
Gary Cooper
John Cornyn
Norris Cotton
Ann Coulter
Alfonse D'Amato
Charles Dawes
Chauncey Depew
Bo Derek
Thomas Dewey
Everett Dirksen
Bob Dole
John Dos Passos
Frederick Douglass
Matt Drudge
John Foster Dulles
Robert Duvall
Will Durant
Clint Eastwood
Dwight D. Eisenhower
Julie Nixon Eisenhower
Mamie Eisenhower
Larry Elder
Jerry Falwell
B.C. Forbes
Malcolm Forbes
Betty Ford
Gerald Ford
William Frenzel
Milton Friedman
Joe Garagiola
James Garfield

List of Speakers Continued

Mel Gibson
Newt Gingrich
Rudy Giuliani
Jonah Goldberg
Barry Goldwater
Phil Gramm
Kelsey Grammer
Ulysses S. Grant
Alan Greenspan
Fiorello La Guardia
Alexander Haig
H.R. Haldeman
Learned Hand
Mark Hanna
Sean Hannity
Warren Harding
Paul Hardy
Angie Harmon
Benjamin Harrison
Paul Harvey
Orrin Hatch
Rutherford B. Hayes
Patricia Heaton
Jesse Helms
Charlton Heston
Eric Hoffer
Oliver W. Holmes Jr.
Sidney Hook
Herbert Hoover
Bob Hope
David Horowitz
Mike Huckabee
Charles Evans Hughes
Robert M. Hutchins
Henry Hyde
Robert Green Ingersoll
Bob Inglis
Laura Ingraham

Bruce Jenner
Herman Kahn
Jack Kemp
Russell Kirk
Jeane Kirkpatrick
Henry Kissinger
C. Everett Koop
Tom Korologos
Charles Krauthammer
Irving Kristol
Lawrence Kudlow
Dan Kuykendall
John Kyl
Alf Landon
Wayne LaPierre
G. Gordon Liddy
Rush Limbaugh
Abraham Lincoln
Heather Locklear
Henry Cabot Lodge
Alice R. Longworth
Kathryn Jean-Lopez
Rich Lowry
Clare Boothe Luce
Henry Luce
Frank Luntz
Douglas MacArthur
Michelle Malkin
Dan Marriott
Jackie Mason
John McCain
Mitch McConnell
William McKinley
Michael Medved
Edwin Meese III
Dennis Miller
Dwight Moody
Rupert Murdoch

List of Speakers Continued

Ron Nessen
Albert Jay Nock
Oliver North
Ted Nugent
Bill O'Reilly
P.J. O'Rourke
Donny Osmond
Sarah Palin
Ron Paul
Boies Penrose
Dennis Prager
Dan Quayle
Marilyn Quayle
Michael Reagan
Nancy Reagan
Ronald Reagan
Thomas Brackett Reed
Don Regan
Elliot Richardson
John D. Rockefeller
Nelson Rockefeller
George Romney
Mitt Romney
Theodore Roosevelt
Karl Rove
Donald Rumsfeld
William Safire
Pat Sajak
Michael Savage
Antonin Scalia
Phyllis Schlafly
Laura Schlessinger
Arnold Schwarzenegger
Norman Schwarzkopf
Brent Scowcroft
Richard Shelby

Richard Nixon
George Shultz
William E. Simon
Alan Simpson
Gary Sinise
Tony Snow
Thomas Sowell
Sylvester Stallone
Ben Stein
Jimmy Stewart
Henry Stimson
John Sununu
Martha Taft
Robert Taft
William Howard Taft
Cal Thomas
Fred Thompson
Strom Thurmond
Jon Voight
Earl Warren
Booker T. Washington
James G. Watt
John Wayne
Caspar Weinberger
William Weld
Christine Todd Whitman
George Will
Walter E. Williams
Wendell Willkie
Henry Wilson
Walter Winchell
Tom Wolfe
Ron Ziegler
Zig Ziglar

Made in the USA
Lexington, KY
25 April 2010